Red, White, and Black Make Blue

EST. 75 1938
YEARS
THE UNIVERSITY OF GEORGIA PRESS 2013

Red, White, & Black Make Blue

INDIGO IN THE FABRIC OF
COLONIAL SOUTH CAROLINA LIFE

Andrea Feeser

THE UNIVERSITY OF GEORGIA PRESS ⟫ ATHENS & LONDON

© 2013 by the University of Georgia Press
Athens, Georgia 30602
www.ugapress.org
Designed by Erin Kirk New
Set in Adobe Caslon Pro
Printed and bound by Thomson-Shore, Inc.
The paper in this book meets the guidelines for permanence
and durability of the Committee on Production Guidelines for
Book Longevity of the Council on Library Resources.

Printed in the United States of America

17 16 15 14 13 P 5 4 3 2 1

Library of Congress Cataloging-in-Publication Data

Feeser, Andrea.
    Red, white, and black make blue : indigo in the fabric of Colonial
South Carolina life / Andrea Feeser. — 1st edition.
        pages cm
Includes bibliographical references and index.
    ISBN 978-0-8203-3817-0 (hbk. : alk. paper) — ISBN 0-8203-3817-6
(hbk. : alk. paper) — ISBN 978-0-8203-4553-6 (pbk. : alk. paper) —
ISBN 0-8203-4553-9 (pbk. : alk. paper)
    1. Indigo industry—South Carolina—History—18th century.
2. Indigo—South Carolina. 3. South Carolina—History—Colonial
period, ca. 1600–1775. 4. Plantation life—South Carolina—History—
18th century. 5. Plantation owners—South Carolina—History—18th
century. 6. Slaves—South Carolina—History—18th century.
7. African Americans—South Carolina—History—18th century.
8. South Carolina—Race relations—History—18th century.
9. Textile fabrics—History—18th century. 10. Clothing and dress—
Social aspects—History—18th century. I. Title.
    HD9019.I32F44   2013
    667'.26—dc23   2013003108

British Library Cataloging-in-Publication Data available

For my family: you were there when things got too blue.

CONTENTS

ACKNOWLEDGMENTS

I have many people and institutions to thank for their contributions to my work. For financial support, I am indebted to Clemson University's College of Architecture, Arts, and Humanities for grants to conduct research in England at the National Archives, the British Library, the London Metropolitan Archives, and the Guildhall Library, and in the United States at the Library of Congress, Duke University's David M. Rubenstein Rare Book and Manuscript Library, the South Carolina Department of Archives and History, the South Carolina Historical Society, the Charleston Archive of the Charleston County Public Library, and the Charleston Library Society. I thank all of the many archivists and librarians who assisted my labor at these institutions as well as those individuals at libraries and museums who helped me secure illustrations for this book. I also received a grant from the South Carolina Humanities Council to create and present with Karen Hall and Kendra Johnson public programs on indigo: these efforts brought me into contact with many people who taught me much about how indigo's history affects the present. Clemson's Art Department, where I am fortunate to work with marvelous colleagues and students, funded photographs taken by Anderson Wrangle for this book. I thank Anderson for his beautiful pictures.

I am grateful for the knowledge I gained from individuals whose lives emerged for me through archival research and from the wonderful scholars whose texts inform this book. I also thank Ralph Bailey Jr. for information about eighteenth-century South Carolina indigo vats, Lydia M. Pulsipher for helping me research eighteenth-century Montserrat, and Harriet Simons Williams for her thoughts about slave John Williams. I am indebted to the people who read my work—especially Peggy Galis, Karen Hall, Erika Stevens, Beth Tobin, and my anonymous reviewers—and to the audiences who listened to papers I delivered at conferences organized by the Society for Economic Botany, the American Society for Eighteenth-Century Studies, the Southeastern American Society of Eighteenth-Century Studies, and the Group for Early Modern Cultural Studies. I learned much about dyes and pigments from the authors who contributed to a book on early modern color that I coedited with Beth Tobin and Maureen Goggin and that Erika Gaffney and Emily Ruskell saw to fruition. I received hands-on experience with dye from Karen Hall—a consummate dyer—and discovered a great deal about eighteenth-century textiles with the help of costume historian and designer Kendra Johnson. Tim Drake gave me an unprecedented opportunity to learn about a specific such textile—the wrap made by Eliza Lucas Pinckney that he owns—and I am indebted to him for sharing that wonderful garment with me.

At the University of Georgia Press, Erika Stevens gave the project its shape and worked with me to develop it even after she left the press. Laura Sutton and especially Regan Huff helped me see the manuscript through to completion, and Rebecca Norton shepherded it through production. Ellen D. Goldlust did wonderful copyediting. Sydney Dupre oversaw many of the book's particulars, and Amanda E. Sharp launched its circulation. Erin Kirk New gave the book its beautiful design, and David Wasserboehr created its handsome map. Nancy Grayson brought my project to the press and I greatly appreciate her support.

I am thankful for those who sustained me as I researched, wrote, and revised this book: Karen Hall, Christina Hung, Kim Kelley, Beth Lauritis, Mary Ann Lawson, Christen Mathis, Jacqueline Mouzon, Jennifer Ransom, Beth Tobin, and all of my family members. Among the latter I am especially grateful to Robert Feeser, Elaine Feeser, Hilarey Bhatt, Tim Factor, and Noah Factor. My husband, Tim, and son, Noah, lived this endeavor with me, and their support means the world to me.

Red, White, and Black Make Blue

INTRODUCTION ❧ Why South Carolina Indigo?

IN THE FINAL STAGE of dyeing with indigo, a dyer pulls the cloth from an indigo bath, exposing the material to oxygen and setting off a chemical reaction that changes the cloth from yellowish-green to blue. Watching the transformation is not unlike watching time-lapse photography of a flower blossoming: one thing becomes another slowly enough to mesmerize and quickly enough to thrill. In short, it seems magical.

To dye something is to stain it, and the effect and affect of a spreading stain can be either troublesome or lovely. The cultivation of indigo has this dual aspect, shaded by a complex and sometimes fraught history in the Americas and especially in South Carolina.

Indigo was a plant before it became a dye, and for its role as a dye, it was grown on plantations and farmsteads in huge quantities in the eighteenth-century Atlantic world. As such, it was a true commodity—a colorant that became a staple in British and European manufactures and a bankable asset that enriched a few at the expense of many while driving segments of industries, primarily textile based, especially in Britain. Blue was the most popular color of the eighteenth century.[1] It symbolized the elite (as in the phrase *blue blood*) and the everyday person (evident in the practice of workers donning blue aprons). It was also the easiest dye to come by and simplest to use. Blue paper wrapped heavily consumed goods such as sugar, and blue fabric covered windows, curtains, and furniture.[2] Blue was especially popular for clothing: on military uniforms, ball gowns, orphans' coats, American Indian blankets, court costumes, slave garments, and sailor attire. Indeed, blue was everywhere: in flowering indigo shrubs that covered swathes of the Caribbean and the American South and in the homes, the workplaces, and the dress of everyone from the most privileged to the least regarded. As a plant that helped determine colonists' fortunes in the New World, it marched steadily across native land, planted and tended by many enslaved Africans and some enslaved Indians, at times an extension of colonial and racial oppression, at other times an equalizer. As a dye, it stained some fabrics that secured status and others that marked servitude. This book answers the question of why blue colored the lives—in both positive and negative ways—of so many different people in the British imperial orbit.

Why Blue?

While visiting the Museum of London, I was captivated by a garment that prominently featured blue: a gorgeous eighteenth-century silk brocade dress alive with a rhythmic dance of flowering vines. In particular, my eyes were drawn to the delicate blue blooms scattered amid the profusion of leaves and petals. For a moment, I felt transported to a field of azure blossoms. My momentary transposition from the world of human creation to the world of nature dissolved as I saw a schoolgirl press her nose against the glass case holding the gown and heard her murmur, "A ghost must be wearing that dress." Thrown into the world of the supernatural by that earnest remark, I looked at the absence the dress enveloped: the display organizers had exhibited the dress without a mannequin—that is, in space, without any visible means of support.

This decision was both strangely congruent and at odds with the didactic organization of the display, for the glass case that held the dress contained some period furniture and several text panels that explained who might have worn such a dress and by whom it was likely created. Thus, viewers like me were provided with both the signs and the absence of the life that once animated the dress and moved among the household objects near it. To some extent, this evidence of the past—recovered as well as concealed—satisfied my conviction that we cannot fully flesh out history and make it supremely knowable. But I also felt haunted by the young girl's observation that the dress was worn by a ghost: I imagined a disembodied presence that wanted to be felt, reaching out to the land of the living from the realm of the dead and trying desperately to say something to those of us on this side of the grave.

As I perused items in the museum gift shop, looking for a souvenir to chase away the ghostly absence, a postcard jolted me. The card pictured another eighteenth-century silk dress awash with blue, but this dress was securely draped around a mannequin. Perhaps in a move to approximate the logic of the empty dress on display—to point toward but not presume to represent completely the wearer of the gown—the model figure was black and devoid of any features except an eighteenth-century coif, also black. Against the probable intentions of the person who staged the photograph, I could not help but read the figure as a woman with black skin. Although eighteenth-century black women clothed in sumptuous silk dresses most certainly existed, such a person was not the ghost I had begun to imagine. The ghost who had started to take shape in my head was white.

Thus began a process of incessant wondering about who had animated this gown and others at the museum. The white woman I had imagined—as well as the black woman who subsequently appeared in my mind's eye—alerted me to the fact that many different people can and do shape a manufactured good's existence. I began to think of the people who give garments life not only by wearing them but also by making them. Today, we frequently view made goods of all sorts as mere extensions of their owners, thinking little about the work of the countless heads, hands, and often hearts that realize the objects of our built environment. The beauty of that eighteenth-century silk dress began a process of reverie and then investigation that has now made it impossible for me to see any made thing, whether produced in earlier times or in our own, without sensing the presence of the item's absent makers. This experience makes it increasingly hard for me unconsciously to consume manufactured goods. My study of the creation of an eighteenth-century English luxury has made me think about some profound human injustices very close to home: Indian land dispossession and slave labor in South Carolina, where I live.

The thread of this trajectory weaves in and out of the blue in the flowers of the garment I first admired, delicate blooms that shuttled me between the natural world and a built environment. Today, many made things are synthetic and are divorced from nature, but in the eighteenth century, the products of men and women almost always began with a natural substance. As I figuratively unraveled the dress to consider the processes that went into its creation, I recognized that two natural substances fundamentally structured the garment: cloth and dye.

Because the dye transformed the silk threads embroidered on the cloth, I took dye as the most basic natural material within the dress, although as I learned about dye, I realized that a great many transformative processes alter it as both a substance that is made and as a product that makes something else change. However, dye remained for me the gown's most elemental substance when I recognized that the blue of the embroidered flowers ultimately inspired my quest. The ambivalence I came to feel about the garment, experienced as enormous aesthetic enjoyment and painful moral judgment, parallels the multivalent aspect of blue: it symbolizes both the heavenly and the melancholy.

The dress's blue flowers owe their color to a shrub that in eighteenth-century South Carolina was often cultivated on land taken from Indians and was processed by thousands of slaves on plantations owned by Britons. South Carolina indigo cultivation and dye manufacture first took place on low country land, where colonists initially settled. As colonists fanned out to establish farms and plantations, indigo, too, spread to the backcountry, the frontier past the tidal zone. Growing the indigo plant and creating dye from it was hard work for all involved: it required a good understanding of natural conditions and dye-making procedures as well as numerous other tasks. Indeed, planting, tending, harvesting, and extracting indigo required great labor and skill. Growers needed to gauge soil and weather conditions and protect plants from weeds as well as pests,[3] and dye manufacturers had to determine when to reduce and dissolve components of the colorant by adding oxygen and lime. All of these efforts were taxing, and during the dye-making phase—which entailed fermentation—labor was noisome as well. The African and occasionally Indian slaves who did almost all of this work certainly endured hardship. Further, because indigo grew successfully in South Carolina's various soils, the plant's cultivation became a major cause of Indian suffering. A great deal of colonial land grabbing took place in areas where colonists planned to grow indigo, especially in the backcountry—more properly called Indian Country and populated by Cherokees and other native groups.[4]

From the mid-1740s until the Revolutionary War, indigo was a major crop in South Carolina, making almost as many fortunes for plantation owners as did rice, the colony's most successful commodity in that era. During its time as a key South Carolina export, indigo's reputation varied: good and bad dye cakes were shipped to England. The very best indigo from South Carolina may well have been employed to dye silk used by London's Spitalfields weavers, whose finest product—embroidered and woven silk like that which I admired at the Museum of London—was coveted for its magnificence. As I pursued this possible transformation of an actual blue flower from South Carolina into a handmade flower on a dress made in London, I discovered many of the activities and experiences that shifted a small piece of nature into what philosopher Hannah Arendt has called "the human artifice."[5] What I learned in the process of my research was both uplifting and revelatory and distressing and difficult to reconcile. Although indigo provided some people with security and pride, it subjected others to loss and suffering.

Conceiving Eighteenth-Century South Carolina Indigo Culture

I explore these intertwined histories by investigating how eighteenth-century South Carolina's indigo culture bound together Britons, sovereign American Indian peoples, and enslaved Africans and Indians. I do so by looking closely at garments, artifacts, written documents, and images that embed within themselves something of the politics of indigo in the period, seeking to uncover what is not clearly visible yet is crucial about the boon and bane that indigo became for those who traded in the plant and its products. Just as invisible oxygen is the key ingredient needed to produce indigo blue, several largely unseen histories are crucial components of colonial South Carolina's indigo story.

To explore the rich fabric that comprises this story, chapter 1 looks closely at indigo-dyed cloth and how it connected persons from different realms in the eighteenth-century Atlantic world. Indigo moved along trade routes and through human hierarchies, marking status while it colored material. The chapter begins with debates about South Carolina indigo's quality and how its largely agreed-upon inferiority determined its primary use in Britain: the manufacture of standard dyed and printed cloth worn by those below the upper echelons at home and abroad. Merchants' interest in provisioning this large body of consumers, in conjunction with far-flung business networks, ensured that indigo-treated textiles showed up on the backs of individuals ranging from British soldiers and Indian warriors to English orphans and South Carolina slaves. However blue may have divided native, white, and black men and women from one another in terms of land and labor in South Carolina, indigo also bound many segments of these populations together with respect to blue textile usage.

Chapter 2 examines how two groups used garments colored by indigo to mark their difference from others. Slaves and Indians received very specific textiles: slaves had clothing fabricated from plain "Negro cloth." Indians also acquired goods made from this material as well as calicoes and especially woolens, which were primarily blue stroud blankets termed *matchcoats*. While many of these items were ready-made and thus standardized, owners at times permitted slaves to wear some simple patterns and to dye and decorate garments; in other instances, slaves stole fancier items of clothing or received them as gifts. Colonists also at times presented Indians with elaborate coats or suits, and Native Americans frequently enlivened their trade cloth with decorations and accessories. Thus, blue fabrics that originally marked slaves and natives as such in white settlers' eyes were rehabilitated to express slave and native agency, sartorial articulations that confounded Anglo-Americans' expectations and perceptions. This chapter studies instances of this phenomenon in the context of African and Indian color symbolism, in which blue has both positive and negative associations, as a means of showing how indigo served as a tool to both degrade and empower black and red people.

Chapter 3 explores how several colonial men emblematic of their peers invested in indigo. Monetary rewards are the most obvious payout these men received from their work, but the dye plant provided other dividends as well. For some planters, growing indigo and selling dye cakes afforded a sense of patriotic pride, since the colonial product ended Britain's reliance on indigo grown by its enemies, France and Spain. In addition, indigo formed part of a plantation culture that enabled successful growers to see themselves as patrician gentlemen of the pastoral tradition. And finally, those who were enamored with plants and prided themselves on their knowledge and understanding of the vegetable world acquired intellectual capital by experimenting with indigo.

Chapter 4 looks specifically at how indigo was tied to land use and acquisition in eighteenth-century South Carolina, particularly as the colony's rice boom faded. Seeking to bolster their planting enterprises with another crop, growers found that indigo suited perfectly: it grew on drier land interspersed among swampy rice fields and flourished in the varied soils of the backcountry. As South Carolina officials sought to offset the rapidly growing slave population by encouraging white settlement, indigo became part of an agricultural incentive to expand the colony, bringing settlers up against and into Indian territory. To a certain degree, troubled relations among Indians and colonists were soothed by trade, which for natives included the acquisition of blue cloth and clothing. Indigo blue became not only a tool for balancing black, white, and native relations but also a wedge between Indians and colonists when incursions into Indian Country became too aggressive.

Chapter 5 explores in detail the relations among native, white, and black peoples on indigo plantations, closely studying the hard labor of growing indigo and extracting the dye. The bulk of this work was performed by enslaved Africans, some of whom came from parts of West Africa where indigo making and dyeing had a long and rich history. The chapter discusses slaves' contributions to South Carolina indigo culture in light of the model of production introduced to the colony from the Caribbean and the modifications made to it by enterprising South Carolinians. These analyses integrate the often-disregarded history of Indian slavery, which is typically dropped from discussions of life in the colony after the Yamassee War of 1715–17, when most—but not all—Indian slaving stopped. Enslaved native men and women lost their homelands as well as their freedom to indigo production.

Chapter 6 counters this dire history with a study of how one native man with possible African blood abandoned the project of turning indigo into gold for one of Britain's most powerful businessmen. Indigo's relationships to land and labor lie at the heart of this investigation, which explores the ways in which the crop was used by Britons in the Southeast to create wealth by working African slaves on land usurped from Indians. In addition, the chapter recounts the means by which one Native American likely pursued his own path as a cultivator in East Florida.

Chapter 7 turns to South Carolina's best-known indigo plantation, which was managed by the young Eliza Lucas (later Pinckney). Lucas has been credited with establishing the plant in the colony, and the chapter uses careful documentary analysis to show the key role played by slaves, particularly Quash (later John Williams), in her indigo-making efforts as well as in the construction and maintenance of a city home for Eliza and her husband, Charles Pinckney.

Material Culture and History

Because this book features analyses of many objects, including letters, maps, prints and paintings, and garments, and because it interlaces varied histories to construct a dense social fabric, my interpretive strategies are informed by scholarly work done on both material culture and the making of history. In the first area, I have been inspired by methods that view objects as dynamic actors in the theater of life.[6] This view makes individuals and objects mutually constitutive and thus gives human products a role in the arena of contemporary events and on the historical stage. Historian Laurel Thatcher Ulrich explores this idea in light of how textiles can structure human relations while providing great insight into the meaning of these interactions,[7] and I am indebted to her point that actual fabric reveals the forces at work within the social fabric.

Several contemporary historians have reflected on history as a made thing, and in this sense, I treat colonial South Carolina's indigo culture as a textile colored blue by the lives of red, white, and black peoples. With respect to history more broadly, I am particularly indebted to Joan Scott's argument that "history is in the paradoxical position of creating the objects it claims only to discover."[8] In making this pronouncement, however, Scott does not intend to suggest that history is merely fiction. I agree with her on this point and support both her account of and call for a means of describing the past that historian and philosopher Michel Foucault names "effective history."[9] Foucault sees such transformation not as the product of destiny or the actions of heroes but as occurring without any known constant or stable agent. History occurs, but it is constructed, made like any human product from whatever is given. As Scott maintains, such a definition of the past—which unravels any absolute conception of the subjects, objects, and even objectives of history—need not throw us into an understanding of time past that is merely subjective and relative. On the contrary, she argues,

> If there is nothing inevitable about the direction of change, it nonetheless happens and it does so because of human intervention, understood not as an assertion of autonomous will, but as discursively situated challenge to prevailing rules and disruption of existing hierarchies. If there are no inherent landmarks or points of reference, this has not prevented humans from establishing them. Indeed the "lesson of history" is that human agency consists of imposing sense, differently and mutably, upon our worlds.[10]

To grasp the fundamental ruptures that mark past from present without resorting to a sense of the essential or absolute, historians historicize both former and current interpretations. In such a conceptual armature, facts "are the data that provide insight into particular interpretive operations," marshaled not only by past persons but also by historians to make sense of experience.[11]

Anthropologist Karl Kroeber argues that Native American myth continually renews culture,[12] which I understand as a form of history that fundamentally changes how we understand the past in relation to the present. Kroeber believes that preliterate societies keep their culture alive through the retelling of myths that adapt to new circumstances and that are incorporated imaginatively and constructively into historical understanding. He maintains that although some people within the Western tradition believe in such a form of world renewal, Indian orators are particularly adept at weaving threads of the past into a social fabric that richly clothes the present. In Kroeber's words,

> Native American mythic retellings, however, normally do not strive to be identical with earlier tellings, not simply because, in oral enactments, no two tellings can be identical but also because the ongoing vitality of preliterate cultures depends on processes of continuous self-renewal. Writing, and, above all, print, seems to release culture from the imperative awareness of the need for continuous self-reconstituting. However, all life forms, especially complex ones such as cultures, survive only by adapting, being capable of change and adjustment to new circumstances. Myths are means for cultural adaptations. Contrary to popular misconceptions of them as mere preservatives of tradition, these narratives are, in fact, an essential discourse technique by which preliterate societies modify, as well as reaffirm, their cultural systems.[13]

Kroeber describes the practice of such modification through an appeal to the work of Mikhail Bakhtin, a linguist who discerned the dialogic dimensions of human interaction, showing that our doings and our understandings of them are shaped by how we make meaning through and with our many interlocutors. Such an approach to understanding can shape how we write history, requiring investigators to find a variety of historical accounts to locate many participants with a range of tales to tell.

My interlocutors, both historical personages and documents of material culture, have helped me write this narrative of eighteenth-century South Carolina indigo culture with red, black, and white amid the blue. I weave into the fabric of colonial South Carolina life the stories of many people, producing a history that I hope Kroeber would term a world-renewing myth. Today's South Carolina is rich and complex, and examining its multidimensional past may help us better understand its multidimensional present.

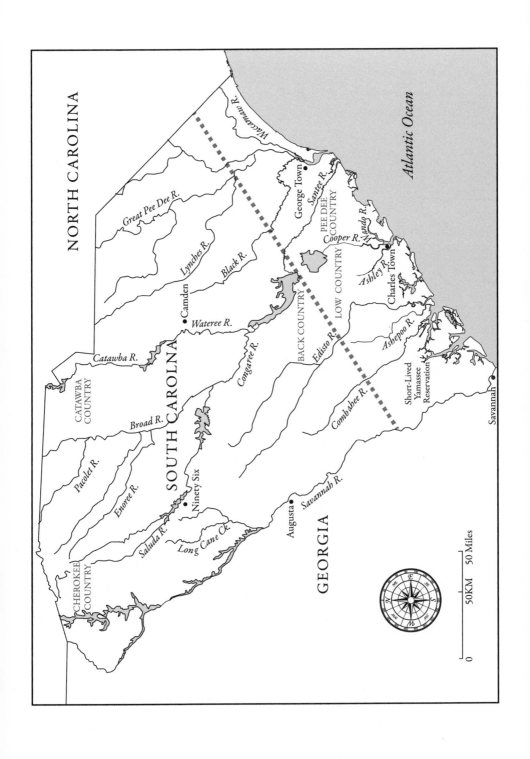

PART I

South Carolina Indigo in British and Colonial Wear

CHAPTER 1 ❧ South Carolina Indigo in
British Textiles for the Home and Colonial Market

ABOUT 250 YEARS AGO in Covent Garden, one of London's prime business and entertainment districts, dyer Barnaby Darley's sign hung prominently among other trade placards.[1] The eye-catching sign features an Indian "queen" in flowing, patterned garb shaded by two scantily clad, male attendants who hold aloft an umbrella. Both wear headdresses of feathers or leaves and reach no higher than the queen's shoulders: the taller of the two is black; the smaller one, clearly a child, is lighter skinned. The sign closely resembles those that hung outside London linen and silk shops, a phenomenon that communicates in a visual, allegorical way the ties among those who colored cloth and those who transformed it into garments. The image also conveys Britons' perceived links—indeed, odd amalgamations—among the peoples of India, Africa, and the Americas: variations on the queen-with-attendants theme show the ruler with feathered headdress and render all of the figures black. This melding of Indian and African is evident in other shop signs that represent a single "black boy" as a dark-skinned child with a bow and arrow and feathers in his hair. Thus, shop placards—specifically those that advertised fabric, dyeing, and clothing—throughout London's business districts mixed and matched pictures of colored people as emblems of colored attire. However inaccurate these representations were, they do communicate two facts: dyes were produced in colonies peopled by those with dark skin, and these individuals wore British fabrics colored with these dyes.[2]

The Indian queen with attendants is thus a strange but powerful illustration, succinctly conveying information and ideas. The Indian queen—shown in most versions of the theme wearing calico, which often contained indigo-dyed designs—represents India, the West Indies (Caribbean), the southeastern North American colonies, or perhaps all three, areas where Britons had grown or were growing indigo on plantations. Regal and proud, she is attended by subservient Africans or Indians (of India and/or the Americas). The stark realities that attended the production of color such as indigo for cloth are obscured in such an image, hidden behind an idealized allegory. The picture of the sovereign Indian masks the actual native people who were alienated from land taken for staple production, and the representation of the small, dark servants veils the real slaves who were worked unsparingly to make indigo. Further, the illustration diminishes the power of Indians and Africans affected by British plantation culture. For example, these peoples in South Carolina had ferociously fought white colonizers: the 1715–17 Yamassee War almost destroyed the colony, and the 1739 Stono Rebellion was the largest slave uprising in Britain's North American holdings. The dyer's trade sign, however, feminizes natives and infantilizes Africans and/or Indians, suggesting that neither is ultimately threatening. In keeping with the goals of a dyer such as Darley, the only message relayed is that indigo and other hues are special and exotic.

That idea certainly had previously held true for indigo: it has been a highly valued dye since ancient times. Although the chemical that produces blue color is found in a number of plants, the indigo genus, *indigofera*, grown in tropical and subtropical climes, secured the best reputation as a dye.[3] However, prior to the late sixteenth century, indigo was not used extensively in Britain or Europe because of the abundance of the blue-producing woad plant. Indeed, in Britain, woad was protected from imported indigo through much of the Middle Ages because woad's growth and manufacture supported many British growers and dyers. Dye made from *indigofera* was a rare luxury item in Northern Europe, used primarily as paint and ink and brought in from the Middle East at great expense.[4] However, the superiority of the dye extracted from *indigofera* caused Europeans to seek to produce their own supplies of the dye and thus end their dependency on foreign imports secured largely via Arab trade networks. Portugal and Spain were the first European countries to procure their own indigo, which came from colonies in warm parts of Central and South America. Other nations followed suit, establishing colonies in tropical and subtropical regions where indigo and other staples grew well. The Dutch manufactured indigo in Indonesia, the British experimented with the crop in India, and the French and British cultivated the plant on various Caribbean islands (notably Haiti, Jamaica, and Montserrat), as well as in some of their warmer North American holdings.

By the eighteenth century, indigo from plantations in the Americas was used extensively, especially to color cloth, which was used by people of all stations for a wide variety of purposes.[5] Because blue was by far the most popular color in Britain in the period,[6] because indigo became a staple that benefited many people within British trade networks, and because the country played a dominant role in eighteenth-century textile manufacture, indigo ended up in enormous amounts of goods consumed by Britons and those with whom they dealt. Although English dyers purchased French and Spanish indigo grown in the Caribbean and Central America, it was a fraught commodity. Foreign dye was expensive, and during the century's many wars, it was available in Britain only when British privateers captured ships that carried it. Indeed, as a product of Britain's great enemies, French and Spanish indigo would have been shunned had it not secured an excellent reputation in London, Britain's central imperial trade hub. In fact, South Carolina indigo—usually called Carolina indigo—was often maligned,[7] much to the consternation of several colonial businessmen with vested interests in the dye.

South Carolina Indigo's Uneven Reputation

Mixed opinion about the colonial staple is starkly evident in several late eighteenth-century exchanges among different experts on indigo. In 1772, an anonymous South Carolina planter, Charles Town–based dye inspector Moses Lindo, and English dyer John Ledyard engaged in a bitter debate about South Carolina indigo. Ledyard published a pamphlet in which he complained about the dye's quality and offered advice to planters for improving the staple. Lindo and the anonymous planter responded with irate letters to the *South Carolina Gazette* disputing Ledyard's claims. The heat that characterizes these documents is also readily apparent in other period texts. South Carolina indigo grower and merchant Henry Laurens produced several accounts of his frustration with the staple's reputation, and a British pamphleteer vented his irritation with a bounty paid on South Carolina indigo.[8] Despite Laurens's and Lindo's efforts, South Carolina dye was broadly seen as inferior to that made on French and Spanish plantations.

Ledyard, an experienced blue-dyer from Melksham in Wiltshire, framed his opinion about South Carolina indigo both in terms of improving a colonial staple and with respect to his needs as a businessman. He distributed his pamphlet widely in Britain and in South Carolina, underscoring his desire to help by offering his text for free, along with hogsheads of lime at cost, because he believed that the substance improved the dye. He thereby set himself up as a benefactor to those he criticized by offsetting his sharp criticism with the supposed means for indigo makers to improve their product. He also promised to purchase South Carolina indigo made according to his instructions.[9]

Ledyard argued that the problem with colonial dye was not the character of the color but instead the volume required: he needed fifteen pounds of South Carolina indigo to achieve the same tones he got from one pound of the Spanish or French colorant, eliminating any financial benefits from purchasing cheaper indigo from the British colony. Ledyard blamed the Carolina dye's shortcomings on the fact that dye makers there allowed their vats to "putrefy," not only compromising the intensity of color in the finished dye but making it stink. Ledyard believed that using English lime rather than lime made in South Carolina from oyster shells would curtail decomposition:

> Now it is very evident that *Putrefaction* is of the greatest prejudice to Indigo, as it destroys (if suffered to continue but a short time) the blue colour contained in it: and as Lime from experience is known to be the only effectual preservative of the Indigo against putrefaction, it seems clearly to follow, that the using of Lime more plentifully in the making of Indigo, would be at least, a probable method to fix and preserve the blue colour from putrefaction, and the injury that necessarily attends to it.[10]

The anonymous planter and Lindo hotly contested Ledyard's assertions about lime. Both writers had expertise with indigo: the planter oversaw the production of the dye, and Lindo knew how to grade it, since he had worked as a dye broker in London before coming to Charles Town in 1756. After settling in South Carolina, Lindo became an indigo inspector and purchased a vessel for shipping dye and other products to London. Respected in Charles Town for his background, Lindo received the official post of South Carolina indigo inspector in 1762.[11] Lindo was thus well positioned to question Ledyard's analysis of and prescriptions for South Carolina indigo. Lindo retorted that when planters tried Ledyard's lime, they found that it spoiled their product. Moreover, Lindo questioned the assertion that foreign indigo provided much better dye, maintaining that I have never met with any Carolina Indigo so very bad: And, that the true value of such Indigo, the produce of this province as I have garbled, sorted and sealed, is in the following proportion; when the best French or Spanish sells at seven shillings the pound, *viz.*

		s.	*d.*
First sort is worth		5	9
CAROLINA,	{Second —	4	2
	Third — —	2	9^{12}

The anonymous planter chastised Ledyard even more harshly, noting that Spanish, French, and South Carolinian indigo producers used essentially the same ingredients and processes and that Ledyard contradicted himself when he asserted that the dyes from different sources differed not in color but only in strength. The planter reminded his readers that indigo was valued not by its provenance but instead by its type (with resulting differences in color, sheen, and texture) and that all of the sources produced the same dye variations, with flora at the top and copper at the bottom. He conceded that because the Spanish and French had been making indigo longer than South Carolinians, the two countries likely made more of the higher-quality dye, but not to the degree that Ledyard claimed. The planter went on to argue that British dyers might not have known the provenance of the indigo they used and might simply have assumed that dye that seemed better was Spanish or French. He chastised Ledyard for dismissing a product grown and made by his fellow Britons and noted that such public critiques might undercut trade of benefit to the mother country as well as promote the purchase of enemy nations' indigo. The planter concluded,

I now take the liberty on my side, to propose a query or two, *viz.*

I. Whether frequent instances could not be produced, where the *best* Carolina Indigo has been picked out, and sold for French, and the *Bad* sold under the denomination of Carolina Indigo, to the great hurt and prejudice of the province?

II. Whether the Blue Dyer has not been supplied with the *bad sort*, and formed his notions of Carolina Indigo?

III. Whether prejudice does not appear to operate with him against Carolina Indigo?[13]

Laurens, an indigo planter and merchant, certainly asked himself the same questions, and he tried an experiment to answer them. In 1772, the same year Ledyard published his pamphlet, Laurens successfully passed off some of his South Carolina product in England as indigo cultivated elsewhere.[14] Because Laurens grew and sold his own as well as others' indigo, he had a vested interest in promoting South Carolina's second staple. By fooling experts in London, Laurens believed, he had not only proved the value of his product but also uncovered hostility to the dye produced on his and other colonists' plantations.[15]

This hostility was evident in pamphlets circulated in Britain and North America at the time of the Revolutionary War. Writing in 1775, one author angrily despaired at British underwriting of colonial planting ventures: "Could not our manufacturers have indigo much better and cheaper from France and Spain than from Carolina; and yet, is there not a duty imposed by acts of parliament on French and Spanish indigo, that it may come to our manufacturers at a dearer rate than Carolina indigo, though a bounty is also given out of *the money of the people of England* to the Carolina Planter, to enable him to sell his indigo upon a par with the French and Spanish."[16]

The writer's irritation must have been exacerbated by colonists' continued resistance to import duties, which had exploded spectacularly in the Stamp Act crisis of the previous decade, with South Carolinians adding their voices to the cacophony of colonial denunciations of taxation. The supposed poor quality of South Carolina indigo must have been very useful to critics of economic legislation that favored colonists, and published condemnations of the bounty paid on South Carolina indigo certainly further lowered metropolitan opinions of the staple.

Although political and economic factors may have fueled prejudices against South Carolina indigo and eighteenth-century indigo made elsewhere was also suspect,[17] contemporary historians generally concur with Ledyard's argument that South Carolina's dye was the poorest of the period, citing both environmental and procedural factors. First, South Carolina's weather and soil were less hospitable for indigo growing than were conditions in more tropical locations. Second, even though the bounty on the staple was supposed to go only to planters who shipped a fine product, Britain had no government-endorsed inspection of the dye, so the bounty was paid on indigo of all grades. Planters therefore had no incentive other than their reputations to make good indigo, and such motivations might inspire Laurens and other indigo planters and merchants who valued civic stature but could not ensure quality across the board.[18]

Despite its questionable reputation, South Carolina indigo was exported to Britain in large quantities, garnering wealth for growers in the colony and supplying dyers and ultimately cloth manufacturers with a blue that tinged many garments.[19] In fact, South Carolina indigo colored the majority of British-made blue cloth since that dye was cheaper and "homegrown."[20] Although French and Spanish indigo certainly dyed expensive, bespoke fabrics produced in Britain and colored material for less elite wear there, costly foreign indigo was not a wise choice to color more common cloth.[21] By the middle of the eighteenth century, a great deal of such fabric was being manufactured, largely in Ireland and England's West Country. Cheaper, lighter, and easier to clean, common cloth was often cotton mixed with silk, wool, flax, hemp, and other materials. Since consumers liked blue and indigo was readily available, economical, and simple to make relatively colorfast, it showed up on a great many everyday garments, accessories, and furnishings. Although nobles and wealthy gentry wore embroidered silks and finely crafted woolens frequently colored with fine dyes, people of lower classes in the British imperial orbit usually wore humbler fabrics typically made with lesser materials.[22] South Carolina indigo was certainly a component of these less privileged individuals' dress, a visible yet unnoticed marker of the plantation economy that girded Britain's empire. Soldiers, sailors, orphans, tradespeople, and even the real Native Americans and slaves obscured behind the fantasy queen and servants of Darley's sign were colored by the colony's blue.

Blue and British Clothing Consumption

Britons would have identified the Indian queen on Darley's sign with a number of native personae but especially with South Asians, because Indian cotton textiles sparked an important shift in British fashion. Chintz, calico, and other colorful printed cotton cloth from the subcontinent were extremely popular in Britain from the end of the seventeenth century to the early part of the eighteenth century. Imported to the British Isles by the East India Company, these textiles were valued for their gorgeous appearance, comfortable feel and drape, lightness in warm weather, and ease of cleaning. Marvels of craftsmanship, their patterns—often botanical—were expertly rendered in rich hues and approximated the look of infinitely more expensive embroidered silks produced in London by Huguenot settlers and their descendants. South Asian fabrics were also cheaper as well as more decorative than the woolens Britons were famous for producing. Because of these qualities, British silk and wool manufacturers lost considerable business to imported Indian cottons and took concerted action to cut them out of the market. Pamphlets accused consumers, especially women, of flights of fashion that undermined the British economy and the livelihoods of their countrymen. Silk workers fomented rebellion and kicked off spectacular riots. And representatives of both the wool and silk industries pushed for legislation, passed in 1720, that forbade the importation of the Indian textiles.

However, clever British cloth makers realized that satisfying rather than frustrating consumer desire was a better tactic, and they began to produce cotton fabric and lighter materials that contained cotton.[23] Further, dyers learned how to approximate Indian patterns through block printing and by printing and "penciling" indigo directly onto cloth.[24] British manufacturers soon were supplying consumers with inexpensive and beautifully colored light fabrics, many decorated with Asian-inspired botanic themes that reflected not only the lure of plants but also the extent to which plants constituted the staples that dominated trade. Many Britons and their customers literally decorated their bodies and homes with visual emblems of how the natural world had been put to work for imperial gain.

A broad section of British society both at home and in the colonies could afford to purchase these fabrics, and the materials' beauty and low cost helped shape ideas about and trends in fashion.[25] Many members of Britain's upper crust came to believe that lower-class people were dressing above their station, fretting that placing a person socially through appearance was becoming increasingly difficult.[26] Dress is typically a very important means of structuring identity and position, as sumptuary laws the world over have demonstrated, and maintaining clear boundaries in social hierarchies preoccupied class-conscious Britons. Participating in sartorial expression through coveted fabrics, long solely a prerogative of the powerful, became an equal preoccupation for less elevated members of society.[27]

New materials and spreading fashion consciousness also helped grow the manufacture and consumption of ready-made apparel in a variety of cloths, although the largest motivating factor in this sector was less benign: the many wars of the eighteenth century, which required outfitting countless soldiers. These wars were fought largely at sea and in the colonies, under varied conditions and in different climates. Thus, woolens and wool mixes along with lighter fabrics figured into what became an expanding matrix of manufactured clothing. The huge numbers of uniforms, shirts, stockings, and other apparel items produced for British soldiers created the supply and manufacturing mechanisms that permitted the relatively cheap production of many sorts of ready-made dress for the population at large.[28] Whereas some groups, such as orphans and slaves, might have very little say over how they were provisioned, Native Americans were often clients with preferences. Warm wool blankets and coats as well as light shirts were among their most desired trade goods. Therefore, merchants with the capital and subcontracting networks necessary to commission the production of a great many clothes as well as the connections needed to secure government contracts drove the outfitting first of soldiers and sailors and then of Britons and their associates the world over.

Following the subcontracting practices of merchants in clothing and cloth provides insight into how cost and value issues reflect on dye usage. Clothing manufacturers found New World indigo abundant and easier to use than many other dyes, and consumers had long associated blue with the regal and heavenly.[29] Indeed, such diverse eighteenth-century primary sources as business records and family portraits demonstrate that the color predominated in the dress of Britons from all walks of life. As the debates about South Carolina indigo's quality suggest, dyers who colored cheaper blue garments would not have used the pricier and scarcer Spanish and French indigo in large quantities, if at all, but instead employed the less expensive and more plentiful South Carolina colorant. Whether coloring fibers, cloth, or clothing, dyers who had large orders to fill would have relied on a blue that enabled them to maximize profit.[30] When producing limited amounts of a luxury material, conversely, dyers would have used a more costly indigo that would have increased the price that could be charged for the material and thus the amount of profit to be made.

The London Foundling Hospital billet books demonstrate in a very physical manner the blue bonds that linked those within the lower elements of eighteenth-century Britain. Recorded in these books are descriptions of children left in the care of the state, and most entries feature not only a written inventory of each child's possessions but also a swatch of fabric from the child's attire to aid in identification should someone attempt to reclaim the child. The squares are made of cheaper cloth, but many are decorated with blue checks, stripes, and floral prints.

The swatch for Foundling 11877, left at the hospital in 1759, is a small patch of "flowered lining"—linen material printed with large, peony-like blue blooms.[31] Upon reflection, it is perhaps not surprising that a piece of indigo-dyed cloth—almost certainly colored by South Carolina indigo, given the item's humble character—would serve as a surrogate for the little girl, for garments were significant possessions and helped shaped individual identities, as remains the case today.

Value with respect to indigo might also be reflected in the civic versus the economic sphere, for patriotism certainly could figure into a dyer's calculations. Since South Carolina indigo was British, producers of clothing made with dye from that source could feel proud of using a "homegrown" product versus one made by a foreign enemy. A 1771 issue of the *Middlesex Journal; or, Chronicle of Liberty*, for example, singled out a Yorkshire merchant and dyer for the distinctive manner in which they supported populist politician John Wilkes, who embodied liberty for Britain's middling classes: "A clothier in Yorkshire has sent Mr. Wilkes up a present of cloth to make his liveries—the patriotic taylor of Leicester-fields has offered to make them gratis; and an eminent dyer in the Borough, not to be behind-hand in patriotism (as the cloth was white) has engaged to dye them of a true blue (and from Mr. Wilkes regard for the American colonies) with Carolina indigo."[32]

Blue Cloth and Clothing for South Carolina's Varied Populations

John Dart, a merchant and the commissary general for South Carolina in the middle of the eighteenth century accumulated a textile inventory that demonstrates just how profoundly blue—particularly South Carolina indigo—literally colored the lives of South Carolina's diverse populace. At both ends of its circulation through British trade networks, indigo passed from Dart's business concerns to those who lived in South Carolina. Indigo seed was distributed via Dart's commissary to settlers headed for South Carolina's backcountry; as a merchant, Dart outfitted wealthy and poor whites, sovereign Indians, and black and native slaves. His 1754 textile inventory, which includes a recently received shipment of merchandise, contains every type of blue cloth and clothing for this spectrum of individuals, in shimmering silk and warm wool, fine cotton and coarse linen. The inventory also shows that Dart carried cloth to be made up into household furnishings or garments for individuals of every station as well as ready-made garments such as a gentleman's dress coat and plain shirts for workers, slaves, and natives.

Dart established himself as a Charles Town wholesale and retail merchant in 1730 and subsequently increased his business and reputation by forming alliances with powerful businessmen, purchasing a plantation, and obtaining political positions. He was part owner of two trade ships with important merchants such as Gabriel Manigault, had a rice plantation with thirty-three slaves, and obtained six commissioner positions. Dart's 1744 will was witnessed by Charles Pinckney, suggesting that Dart was close to a key grower and promoter of indigo and one of the colony's most respected individuals. Contact with such prominent men as Manigault and Pinckney would have provided Dart with knowledge about what British textiles suited Charles Town's finest, while his position as a planter and politician would have kept him abreast of Indian affairs, giving him an understanding of what slaves and natives required. His 1754 inventory is filled with British fabric and garments that would have supplied these people, and some of it is blue, undoubtedly dyed with South Carolina indigo, which had steadily made its way to England in bulk since 1747.[33]

The inventory contains yards of woolens, inexpensive cottons and cotton mixes, and coarse linen as well as ready-made clothes in these materials. "Negro cloth," or plains, and Yorkshire cloth, all woolens, appear both as yardage and in some as ready-made jackets, trousers, shirts, and coats. Cotton (often calicoes) and coarse linen osnaburg show up as yardage intended for shirts, shifts, and handkerchiefs. Many of these items are described as solid blue or with blue stripes and checks, while the calico likely sported blue floral designs. Legislation enacted in 1735 and folded into the 1740 Slave Code makes it clear that these lower-end goods in Dart's inventory would have dressed slaves: slaves were permitted to wear "negro cloth, duffels, coarse kearsies, osnabrigs, blue linen, checked linen or coarse garlix or calicoes, checked cottons or scotch plaids."[34]

That these fabrics and clothes would have also dressed natives is evident from a 1751 document created to establish payment in goods for deerskins hunted by Cherokees.

A Blanket	3 Bucks or 6 Does
2 Yards Strouds	3 Bucks or 6 Does
A Garlix Shirt	2 Do. or 4 Does
Osnbrigs, 1 Yard	1 Doe Skin
1 Pr. of Hose	1 Buck and one Doe, or 3 Does, &c.
Handkerchiefs of India	2 Bucks
Ditto, common	Ditto
2 yrds stript Flannen	2 Bucks or 4 Does
Fine Rufel Shirts	4 Bucks or 8 Does
Callicoes	2 Bucks or 4 Does
Callicoes	Ditto, 1 Buck and 1 Doe, or 3 Does
Fine Ribands	1 Buck 2 Yards, or 4 Does[35]

Many blue woolens in Dart's inventory surely served native clients as blankets, matchcoats (mantles), or flaps (fabric hung between the legs and belted at the waist), and although the trade list does not specify the colors of the calicoes, shirts, and ribbons, many must have contained blue decoration because of the color's great popularity. The trade document and inventory show that Indians were trading skins that had formerly comprised the bulk of their clothing and supplanting them with British manufactures, including those dyed with indigo.

❧ ❧ ❧

The swatch from the London Foundling Hospital not only physically indexes a life now past but does so for a London foundling as well as a South Carolina slave and a sovereign Native American. All three of these people could have worn garments made from the same cloth, with heavy-headed blue blossoms decorating their bodies. All might have been physically and literally wrapped in a material manifestation of Britain's use of plants, places, and people for profit.

While slaves and Native Americans did not profit from the South Carolina indigo that dyed such cloth, the blue fabric provided them with opportunities to convey their significance. South Carolina's enslaved and native populations at times used sartorial expression as a means of communicating agency and power. Blue grown in the colony was a part of this significant and very meaningful form of dress.

CHAPTER 2 ⅋ South Carolina Indigo in the
Dress of Slaves and Sovereign Indians

TWO LATER EIGHTEENTH-CENTURY IMAGES of African and American
Indian women—the former visual and the latter textual—provide glimpses of
how black and native people adopted and adapted English cloth to suit their
needs and interests. The first image is an illustration by English artist and poet
William Blake for John Stedman's *Narrative of a Five-Year Expedition against
the Revolted Negroes of Surinam, 1772–77* that depicts largely African females and
their children about to be sold into slavery (illus. 1). The second is a description of Cherokee women by Lieutenant Henry Timberlake, an English soldier
who spent three months living in a Cherokee town and who accompanied three
important Cherokee warriors to London in 1762. Blake's picture shows five
African women wearing strings of beads at their necks and just below their knees
and floral printed cloth wrapped around their waists to make short skirts.[1] Given
the date, it is safe to say that the material is English calico. Timberlake similarly
describes calico and beads in the dress of Native American females: the cloth is
fashioned into "a little short waistcoat," decorated by the beads. According to the
soldier, Cherokee women also wore long skirts of fabric wrapped around their
waists and dressed their hair "with an incredible quantity of silk ribbands, of
various colours."[2] These portrayals of black and Native American women show
similar materials employed differently and indicate that while both Africans
and Indians valued foreign trade beads and cloth, they used these manufactured
goods to express unique, indigenous sartorial values. Other visual and verbal
records suggest that the natives of Africa and North America's Southeast, like
their white contemporaries, used adornment to cover what should not be seen
and enhance what should. Unlike the orphaned girl represented by a swatch of
blue floral cloth in the London billet book, who would have been covered from

neck to ankle, African and Cherokee women were not completely obscured by British calico. Nevertheless, notions of modesty and beauty and the use of fabric in dress link these disparate people, all of whom might have worn a sign of plantation culture in the form of blue flowers colored with South Carolina indigo.

South Carolina indigo–blued cloth operated not only as an index of Britain's conquest of plants, people, and place but also as a space of pleasure and power. This chapter investigates this phenomenon by considering how clothing functions as a means of social control as well as a form of agency, exploring sartorial expression among eighteenth-century Africans, African Americans, and American Indians, for whom blue possessed positive symbolic meanings.

Dress in the British Financial and Moral Economies

Whites involved in trade with Africans and Indians were often puzzled and sometimes disturbed by how those native to Africa and the Americas adorned themselves. In addition to shock at the degrees of undress among Africans and Native Americans, whites also expressed alarm at the corporeal decoration favored by these other peoples: African scarification and teeth filing as well as Indian tattooing and face and body painting. Further, when exchanging manufactured goods for slaves or when trading other commodities with Africans and Indians, European and British explorers and merchants were regularly confounded by the value their clients placed on beads, trimmings, and other items of ornamentation. For example, Dutch arrivals on Africa's Gold Coast, like their predecessors the Portuguese, were surprised to find that the Akan people equally valued the figurative trinkets they made and wore whether they were fabricated from precious metal or wood, leather, and beads. These worn objects, called fetishes by Europeans, disgusted and intrigued whites, who linked the power Africans ascribed to the items to idolatry and ignorance. To foreigners in Africa, gold held supreme value, and people who attached anything but secular significance to it and any other earthly substance were backward. Westerners disdained Africans' devotion to things but benefited from what were perceived as black people's misguided attachments: such individuals were easily "fooled" into exchanging supposedly worthless objects such as beads for "valuable" gold. A similar financial and moral economy prevailed in Europeans' dealings with

North American Indians, who also accepted beads, among other goods, for something else whites greatly valued: land.[3] The value and meaning that Africans and Indians attached to beads and other types of adornment were lost on many of the European people who engaged natives, and to this day, many Westerners ridicule or dismiss those who develop intense attachments to things, particularly of a sartorial nature.[4]

In Western thought, fetishism—the belief that an object instantiates sacred, sexual, or economic power—is often linked to Karl Marx's nineteenth-century theory about the lure of commodities and Sigmund Freud's twentieth-century notion of sexual fixations. However, the idea of the fetish arose in the early modern era and crystallized through interactions among whites and the native peoples with whom they traded and whom they colonized as capitalism arose and then became entrenched. Although the fetish concept today speaks to any individual's supposedly inappropriate deep connection to a physical thing, it initially reflected Europeans' fear of and fascination with indigenous others' profound and close relationships to material objects. Despite the fact that desired and tangible goods circulate through capitalism—the economic system that came to link many Westerners with natives—it is fundamentally structured by abstractions, with money and credit functioning as markers for things and services.[5] Although the eighteenth century certainly continued to feature life experiences in which Westerners created objects that they valued highly, labor and consumption became increasingly divorced: people worked for and produced goods for others in exchange for payment (unless those people were enslaved). In the British context, such a growing detachment from made things was furthered by Protestantism's iconoclasm and its work ethic, which favored accumulation for stability as a moral imperative rather than extreme expenditure to demonstrate power through ostentation (a condition ascribed to "decadent" Catholicism). These forces in Britain constrained but by no means contained manifestations of sartorial excess and functioned as a manner of ascribing values to clothing and appearance. When attire seemed inappropriately to embody power—as when Africans festooned themselves with fetishes, Indians decorated their faces and bodies with bright vermillion, and the British poor aped their betters by wearing brightly colored floral cotton—higher-status Britons infantilized or demonized the transgressors, thus perpetuating the prevailing sense of propriety and maintaining authority.

Prior to the 1700s, British sumptuary laws rather than ridicule corrected "inappropriate" fashion, but mercantilism and burgeoning capitalism sought new clothing markets and contributed to the demise of these legal restraints. As early as the late seventeenth century, London writers Bernard Mandeville and Nicholas Barbon argued that however immoral luxury might be in principle, it bettered society as a whole by motivating people to work for money to spend on finery. Mandeville summarized this thinking when he opined that fashion was the means by which individuals sought to raise their standing and that "it is this, or at least the consequence of it, that sets the Poor to Work, adds Spurs to Industry, and incourages the skilful Artificer to search after further Improvements."[6] The seeds of this argument are reflected in musings of Adam Smith, the great eighteenth-century British champion of trade and consumption. Believing that suffering could be alleviated through the pursuit of personal gain via financial transactions, Smith specifically denounced sumptuary laws and other restrictive measures on individual spending.[7] For eighteenth-century Britain and its empire, trade in and consumption of adornment was thus fraught: attire opened doors for all to pursue the pleasure and power of self-fashioning and for some to achieve wealth in the business of clothing people; at the same time, however, it created the possibility of blurring and crossing boundaries between social identities.

Clothing: Social Control and Agency

Although British sumptuary laws were defunct by the eighteenth century and protectionist legislation that concerned clothing such as the early eighteenth-century ban on Indian cotton failed, Britons of means who cared deeply about the cost and appearance of attire found other ways to restrict what less privileged individuals could wear. In South Carolina, such social control was attempted through several different types of documents and official practices. First, various trade agreements with Indians specified how many deerskins natives had to provide to acquire particular items of dress. Second, governors and other colonial leaders made decisions about what types of clothing should be gifted to native allies. Finally, the 1740 Slave Code specified the types of fabric that slaves could wear and how much their masters could spend to clothe those in bondage. Slaves as a group of consumers had no power to affect what they wore, although some individual slaves and their owners transacted privately to accommodate slaves' needs and desires, and some hardworking and loyal slaves received better clothing for their efforts.[8] Native Americans had more power to affect the type and quality of materials and clothing they acquired. When South Carolinians wanted possessions or protection from neighboring Catawbas, Cherokees, Creeks, or other indigenous people, merchants and traders felt pressured to provide the goods Indians favored. Indians in the South Carolina Piedmont forced traders to stock very specific goods: natives in one area required large blue and red beads, whereas those in a neighboring region would accept only small black and white ones.[9]

This emphasis on discrimination and distinctiveness among slave and Indian dress has parallels with sartorial expression in England, where clothing was an index of burgeoning capitalism's appeal to human desires as well as a vehicle for and sign of power. The South Carolina indigo–dyed livery proudly produced by an English tailor and dyer for John Wilkes discussed in chapter 1 may not have been worn with pride on its completion, since by the late eighteenth century, much of the English populace disdained livery. Although smart looking with its characteristic decorative trim, livery directly announced the wearer's servile status. Because much common dress from the seventeenth century forward copied aspects of wealthy persons' attire—the cut of clothing for members of the upper and lower classes had become similar, and printed cottons resembled rich embroidered silks—society's less privileged sought clothing that made them look more like their betters and feel fashionable.[10] Those who wore livery in Britain could not escape their class standing, and in one notable instance, a person lost his life because he shamed a livery-clad servant. In 1751, a liveried man whipped and then shot a youth who insulted his appearance: the servant had compared the young man to a dog, and the victim responded, "I am not so much like a Dog as you, for I wear my own Coat, and you wear your Master's."[11] By this time, British female servants were wearing their own clothes rather than uniforms,[12] so liveried working-class men particularly stood out; at a time when many people were interested in social mobility and sought to veil their origins through attire, standing out via clothing could be humiliating. In the previous century and during the Renaissance, when livery evolved, men and women took pride in wearing clothing that associated them with wealthy families.[13] By the eighteenth century, however, uniforms were more popular when they spoke to the wearers' stature—for example, if a soldier's dress distinguished him as an officer. Indeed, uniformity and lack of distinction characterized the usual dress of slaves, the least valued members of society. Livery became an important dress item for slaves in the British colonies, visually separating house slaves from field hands.

If livery was meant to mark ownership while suggesting magnificence—in England, that of the master; in the colonies, that of the slave—the vast majority of British slave clothing was intended to provide little more than minimal protection from the elements. In South Carolina, as elsewhere in the British possessions, masters might dress their house slaves in nice clothes either to reflect the tastefulness of their homes or out of genuine affection for those with whom they had closest contact. However, planters chiefly provisioned field hands with clothes for survival: typically cloth for a single set of clothes for summer and another for winter, with a blanket every three years.[14] Some slaves had shoes and stockings, although many did not, and others received caps or handkerchiefs to bind around their heads.[15] South Carolina slaves, especially children, were frequently naked or barely dressed and regularly wore cloth that was inappropriate for the season, poorly made, and/or poorly fashioned into garments.[16] Indeed, some slaves received material rather than ready-made clothes and were expected to create their own attire. In many cases, slaves preferred this approach because when plantation mistresses and their female helpers or hired tailors did the work, they tended to fabricate stock items and to have little interest in producing a good fit.[17] Most slave clothing was made from inexpensive, coarse, and dull fabric, although South Carolina's 1740 Slave Code made some room for variety, specifying the particular cheap materials that planters could buy and permitting some solid colors and patterns, chiefly checks and stripes.[18] Cost-conscious planters eager to profit from their staples, including indigo, maximized gains by keeping investments in slaves low, so clothing was viewed as a necessity, not as ornamentation. Some masters might consider issues of comfort and pride, but only within economic reason.

As free people who at times transacted with whites on equal footing, natives typically found themselves better positioned to get the type of attire they wished, although they sometimes fell victim to unscrupulous traders. From their initial contact with British colonists, Native Americans were impressed with cloth and clothing manufactured in Britain. Much precontact Indian garb was time-consuming to make: animal pelts had to be cleaned, cut, and sometimes sewn, and garments made from plant fibers and feathers passed through some of these processes along with many others. Indians found that when they killed deer for meat (a necessity), they could get a side benefit by exchanging the skins for pre-made shirts and shifts as well as lengths of cloth and blankets that were easily wrapped and belted to form flaps and matchcoats. Native-sewn articles such as leggings were generally easier to make from cloth than hide, and decorative items were also simpler to attach to fabric. Moreover, patterned material pro-vided ready-made decoration that could be further enhanced. Cloth therefore eased the process of achieving a fine appearance, and because Indians acquired fabric in a variety of weights, they could prepare for temperature fluctuations and make garments that dried more readily than did fur and leather.[19]

While Indians favored British materials that enabled them to enhance their clothing—woolens such as stroud and duffel for flaps, leggings, and matchcoats; cotton and linen mixes for shirts and shifts; all sorts of "trinkets" (as traders often termed silver and brass jewelry as well as buttons, bells, beads, and rib-bons)—none of these goods radically changed Indian conceptions of attire.[20] Instead, these items translated existing forms of and ideas about clothing and personal decoration into new media. Although African slaves and their North American–born children had more difficulty affirming their sartorial culture in foreign materials, they, too, did so. As part of the plantation complex that con-sumed native land and bound black and red slaves, South Carolina indigo was also part of dress strategies through which Africans, African Americans, and Indians styled themselves as potent beings with deep attachments to indigenous experience as well as an astute understanding of colonial life.

Southeastern American Indian Sartorial Expression

Southeastern American Indians, including those in South Carolina, who clothed themselves in part with blue British fabric drew on a range of materials in vari-ous colors to protect themselves from the elements, facilitate necessary activities, communicate information about their standing, and please themselves. These qualities might or might not overlap and could change based on the situation. Although natives of the region shared basic commitments to certain sartorial materials and forms (for example, cloth as flaps) as well as functions and tastes (such as ease of movement while retaining modesty), Indian communities had stylistic preferences, and individuals within these communities could exercise some freedom in self-fashioning. Generalizations about the effects of South Carolina indigo on native garb and decoration must, therefore, recognize that southeastern natives' dress was not uniform.

Many North American Indians, including those throughout the Southeast, had traditions of rich color symbolism that highlighted the importance of white, red, and black, with white sometimes represented by light blue and black sometimes represented by dark blue. For many native peoples, white embodied peace and harmony, red instantiated passion and war, and black evoked absence or death.[21] Drawing on this symbolism, Indians could convey a great deal through worn decoration and objects: when mixed with meaningful patterns, white, red, and black body paint and beads announced peaceful or aggressive intentions. Warriors with red and black war paint visually embodied their mighty wrath, whereas wampum belts sewn with largely white beads conveyed peace among allies.

The materials that carried such meaningful, communicative color—originally paint made from plant, mineral, and animal matter along with beads made from shells—were thus extremely important to natives, and when European and British versions of these items were offered to Indians through trade, they became highly prized. Mere fripperies for Westerners, vermillion and glass beads possessed a richness and luster that amplified for Indians the power and meaning of their colorful appearance.[22] Eighteenth-century southeastern natives conceived of themselves in relationship to all things (whether animate or inanimate in Western terms) and sought balance between opposing forces (versus Europeans' and Britons' pursuit of good over evil). Therefore, dress items were not mere decoration but part of assemblages (comprised of anything deemed necessary) through which Indians effected proper relations. Hairstyles, tattoos, painted patterns, ornament, and clothing all formed part of a network of signification that helped achieve balance, and though the means might not be good in Westerners' eyes—as when a vermillion-painted warrior killed a colonist to avenge a clan member shot by a white person—natives perceived the end as necessary. Such deep cultural misunderstanding shot through exchanges between Britons and Indians, for just as the British found natives' love of beads ridiculous, Indians found whites' belief that they could truly own land inconceivable.

Since light blue could stand in for white and dark blue for black, blue could convey a very wide range of beliefs and express varied conditions.[23] In the cosmology of the Cherokees, who populated the northern part of South Carolina at this time, blue could be linked to a very particular set of meanings. For eighteenth-century Cherokees as well as many of their descendants, what native healer J. T. Garrett calls "the right way of relationship" was and remains a journey of all things. This relationship is conceived as a circle (representing balance) containing a cross whose arms point north, south, west, and east; this image conveys an idea of time in which past, present, and future continually inform one another.[24] Each direction is associated with a color aligned with "life values" as well as plant medicine that can help actuate these values. The east is yellow or red and associated with family, the heart, and the spirit. The south is white or green and tied to outdoor experience and nature. The west is black and connected to the setting sun and moon as well as to internal illness that affects physical experience. And the north is light and dark blue as well as purple and is attached to the winds, cold, and calm, reflecting an emphasis on the mind and breath.[25]

While Cherokees saw color as a clear embodiment of experience linked to proper relationships, it opens out onto sets of associations and qualities rather than narrowly establishing meaning. For example, only some plants associated with north medicine contain blue coloration, and only one animal connected to the practice has some relationship to the color: the hawk, which can be seen soaring in the blue daytime or the purple evening firmament. The animal most firmly allied with the blue north is the deer. Garrett maintains,

> Other than the hawk circling in the sky, the deer is the animal that probably best represents the North Direction. To the earlier Cherokee the deer was considered sacred as a cunning and sensitive animal in the forest. It seemed to have an awareness and connection to the Universal Circle that hunters would learn to follow in learning to be excellent at their skill. The deer, or *a wi*, was honored and prized for its soft skin. The deerskin was treated and used in a sacred way, as a wrap for crystals and "to keep special things as part of our Medicine bundle." Everything about the deer was treated with sacred respect so that even the venison hunters were specially trained in just the right way to take the life of a deer.[26]

Thus, a great many objects, plants, beings, places, and states might be associated directly or indirectly with blue, which also designated one of the seven Cherokee clans. Rather than dilute what blue could convey, this condition makes its communicative abilities complex and rich, pointing to a set of meanings that suggest acuity and self-possession as well as defeat and illness.[27]

Given that Cherokee and other southeastern natives sought balance, their sartorial expression not surprisingly included a mix of differently colored materials, with certain hues dominating to extend or augment a state or quality aligned with a path established to secure correct relations. Such an emphasis on purpose need not have excluded the pleasures of individual design and creative expression or practical concerns of comfort and ease. This emphasis does suggest, however, that Indian leaders' attire would have been a primary vehicle for communicating and achieving desired objectives when engaging in diplomacy. Indeed, many native leaders wore clothing gifted to them by British politicians during meetings. Because Indians perceived the foreign attire as embodying connection and attachment, such sartorial display functioned as a profound material index of commitment.[28]

When they wore native dress in dealings with Britons, Indian leaders could convey many more meanings, although white interlocutors, even those who had some understanding of native culture, often did not perceive them. However, Indians involved in diplomacy used native forms of dress to convey what they saw as the proper path. English clothing items—some blue with South Carolina indigo after the dye became a key export to Britain—constituted an important element of this array. Although filtered through British eyes and modes of reception, this condition is evident in an English popular print representing a key Cherokee statesman and two of his warriors (illus. 2).

The 1765 color print by George Bickham was published in London three years after the Indians traveled to England to cement peace with Britain after the Anglo-Cherokee War. A work with many functions—documentary, commemorative, and semisatirical—it represents Ostenaco, Cunne Shote, and Woyi with William Shorey, the Indians' interpreter, who died en route, as well as a dog. Text below the figures names the men (inaccurately in the case of the natives) and describes them briefly as well as colorfully: the ghostly looking Shorey is said to have been poisoned (he in fact died of pneumonia), and the brilliantly dressed Indians are noted for their expertise with the "War Whoop," the peace pipe, and scalping. Represented through contrasts—in the text by turns savage and peaceful, and visually through largely idealized faces at odds with their dramatic and strange attire—the Cherokees of Bickham's work embody the extremes with which whites identified them.[29] British newspapers were filled with accounts of the warriors' visit to England, detailing not only the places and entertainments the visitors experienced (including a spectacle at popular Vauxhall Gardens and an audience with the king) but also the Cherokees' appearance, which was always described with fascination, whether shaded by disgust or admiration.[30] While such value judgments shaped Britons' representations of the natives, the clothing and decoration worn by the Cherokees in the print are consistent with many other written and visual records of the period: the natives wear face paint and elaborate hairstyles, jewelry and belts, and matchcoats, shirts, and leggings similar to those in other accounts of the visitors as well as of their contemporaries.[31]

Each of the Cherokees wears a combination of blue, red, white, and gold. Gold and silver lace and trim were important luxury adornments on eighteenth-century British and Indian attire. Their shine conveyed material wealth to Britons and notions of spiritual power in traditional native cosmology,[32] and Bickham likely made the trim gold in his print because silver would have been harder to depict vibrantly. Gold gorgets hang from the natives' necks, and they wear white leggings and fine versions of the white linen shirts that appear on many Indian trade lists. These three items were also worn by British men: the jewelry was a vestige of armor gifted to distinguished combatants; the shirts were a male dress staple; and the leggings were worn either by farmers or soldiers copying Indian garb (a practice that George Washington endorsed beginning in 1758 to ensure comfort and ease of movement).[33] Red appears in Ostenaco's long belted vest and footwear, Cunne Shote's matchcoat, and Woyi's belt; blue shows up on Cunne Shote's vest and on the matchcoats of the two natives flanking him. Ostenaco's matchcoat is a rich French blue, Woyi's coat is a dusty grayish blue, and Cunne Shote's vest is a sparkling aquamarine. Blue is thus the dominant hue in the assemblage, particularly for Ostenaco. While each person wears a pleasing balance of gold, white, red, and blue, large expanses of blue enfold the two side figures and wrap around the center of the middle individual. Other images of Ostenaco (by Joshua Reynolds) and Cunne Shote (by Thomas Parsons) confirm that the two warriors wore matchcoats on their visit.[34] Given that their trip occurred when South Carolina indigo was near the apex of its boom, the Indians' blue garb was almost certainly colored by the colony's dye. In combination with shining ornament and the vibrant color contrasts of other fabric and paint, the indigo blue mantles must have functioned for the natives as a kind of overarching frame, a means to reveal while containing energy. So while not calm in the sense of blue north medicine, the Cherokees' indigo matchcoats suggest an attitude of girded strength. Insofar as these meanings resonated with the British idea of the flowing cape as a royal emblem, it is easy to see why Londoners often referred to the Cherokees as "kings." In part through British blue, produced by a colonial staple that spread into the far reaches of the empire's territory, Ostenaco and his warriors communicated self-possession and power.

South Carolinian African and African American Sartorial Expression

Colonial South Carolina's slaves came primarily from West African cultures that resembled those of the southeastern Indians in that dress and ornamentation were highly varied while sharing some principal elements. Stripped of their native attire—indeed, at times shipped to North America entirely naked[35]—these enslaved Africans had much less freedom than sovereign Indians did to fashion meaningful sartorial expression that conveyed indigenous values. Nevertheless, slaves indexed their African heritage through one key dress element—the head wrap—and via a hybrid aesthetic in which blue could communicate African concepts of power and protection.

Cloth and beads of varied hues and design had (and have) great importance in Africa. Beads at times functioned as money,[36] and both cloth and beads were bartered from early in the continent's recorded history. Indigenous cloth made from cotton and other plant as well as animal fibers and beads made from shells, bones, and seeds were not only important in African dress and personal adornment but enabled Africans to acquire other prized items through trade. Muslims were among the first outsiders to exchange wares with African peoples, and the spread of that faith across the continent affected patterns of attire, with men and women using cloth to cover larger areas of their bodies.[37] However, although most Africans used some amount of fabric for purposes of modesty and delight, their stratified societies initially made royals the largest consumers of cloth as prestige items. When Europeans and subsequently Britons began trading with Africans in earnest in the fifteenth century, fabric and beads largely accrued to leaders, who incorporated them into rich and complex sartorial displays to signal their power.[38] As trade with Westerners became a key component of African economies, Africans of all stations desired and acquired foreign materials. By the eighteenth century, Britons at trading stations along Africa's western coast were exchanging beads, cloth, and other durable goods for slaves.[39]

Africans never devalued their own manufactures and sought markets for their beautiful fabrics.[40] At the same time, however, they embraced foreign beads and cloth for how both lent themselves to furthering indigenous values and taste in adornment. Some West African cloth makers became famous for their wares, which were not only expensive but also instantiated wealth and prestige. For example, even today among the Hausa of Nigeria, deep blue indigo-dyed wrappers, further darkened with powdered indigo beaten into the material to produce a metallic sheen, announce a man's economic and social power.[41] Color also played a key role in Africans' admiration for Western fabric. Although many African peoples produced gorgeous green, yellow, and blue dyes, they often had difficulty making a satisfactory red, so they frequently unraveled foreign cloth to obtain red thread.[42] Bead color also had significance for Africans: foreign glass came in a wide array of hues, simultaneously producing visual pleasure, conveying meaning, and helping to achieve desired effects. Like Indians, Africans ascribed power to objects fabricated with significant materials. What Westerners derided as fetishes were typically made with beads, fabric, and other items considered important and were often worn or incorporated into clothing and symbolically color coded. Fascinated foreigners produced many accounts of these objects that attest to their varied appearances and uses. Some West African women and children wore strands of colored beads—like the slaves pictured in Blake's print—or nets embellished with beads and other items to protect them from harm.[43]

That blue was often an important ingredient in these amulets is suggested by archaeological work at North American slave sites, where blue beads are commonly found. Work conducted by Linda France Stine, Melanie A. Cabak, and Mark D. Groover not only demonstrates that the presence of blue beads can establish the location of eighteenth-century slave environments but also connects the importance of blue in Africa to elements of African American culture in South Carolina and Georgia. Drawing from narratives of ex-slaves, interviews with contemporary Gullahs (descendants of slaves from the South Carolina and Georgia Sea Islands known for their African-inflected culture), and African American authors committed to historical memory, the archaeologists argue that modern and contemporary low country blacks' association of blue with protection resonates with findings of slaves buried with blue-beaded amulets.[44] Testimony shows that well into the twentieth century, slave descendants carried personal charms, most of which were blue, and some Gullahs still paint door and window trimmings blue to scare off evil spirits.[45] Roger Pinckney, a contemporary specialist on Gullah folk culture, maintains that slaves trimmed their dwellings with remnants from indigo vats,[46] and because African indigo-dyed cloth was surely known by many of the black slaves brought to South Carolina who cultivated the staple, blue and perhaps the indigo plant itself had a role in South Carolina slaves' self-fashioning.

Charged with caring for their clothing and sometimes with making it, some slaves certainly valued blue items they received and even went out of their way to produce related clothes, mending dull whitish-brown Negro cloth attire with patches of blue or even dying drab garments blue. Given the link between the color and protection for many Africans and their American descendants, such blue clothing was at times symbolic in addition to visually satisfying. That aesthetic appearance was important to many South Carolina slaves is apparent in documents that record their activities on Sundays, when they were meant to rest. Written texts by baffled, amused, or indignant whites describe slaves wearing their best attire and worshipping, singing, dancing, and playing games. These reports often belittle Sunday slave dress as gaudy, mismatched, and foolishly self-important.[47] However, one visual document of slaves' finer attire, painted around 1790 by a South Carolina plantation owner, provides a dignified and sensitive portrayal of slaves and records their important use of the head wrap, a key retention of African dress (illus. 3).[48] The painting shows twelve slaves—seven men, four women, and one whose gender is unidentifiable—gathered by their cabins to participate in what appears to be a game or dance. Two males make music with drums and an instrument like a banjo, while two women holding cloth and a man with a stick appear nimbly to step in time. Most of the clothing in the painting is blue, and because South Carolina indigo dyed cheap colonial wear at the time, the staple is indexed by the image.[49] One man wears dark blue breeches, two men wear deep blue jackets, two other men wear faded blue jackets, one woman wears a light blue dress, and two women wear blue-checked scarves over their shoulders. One of these two, another woman, and two of the men wear blue-checked scarves wrapped around their heads. Blue is thus an integral part of the head wrap, which scholars agree comes from Africa.[50] Six of the twelve figures wear head wraps, a corporeal marker of their culture that powerfully illustrates that however much black slaves were forced to accommodate their white masters' desires, they were not fully stripped of their heritage and their humanity. Despite the fact that the slaves' clothes are stock items (manufactured either in Britain or on the plantations), the color enlivens garments that appear looked after, neatly arrayed, and proudly worn. Although the indigo blue signifies that the slaves were physically bound to a staple they cultivated, it also speaks to the fact that these enslaved people cared for and protected their bodies with this color.

The Blue Designs of Slaves and Natives

Anonymous slaves and sovereign natives in South Carolina relayed much about themselves through clothing that featured indigo. In a 1770 issue of the *South Carolina and American General Gazette*, a planter ran an ad for a runaway slave from Angola. The slave was described as wearing a suit of white Negro cloth with "some blue between every seam, and particularly on the fore part of the jacket, a slip of blue in the shape of a serpent."[51] Through this indigo-dyed decoration, the slave marked his clothing with the creature Africans took to be an intercessor with ancestors as well as a symbol of fertility.[52] This visual emblem thereby connected the man to his past and culture as well as to his power to keep his people alive into the future.

At roughly the same time, the Ogilvie family (see chapter 3) acquired several Cherokee dress items, including an ornamented cap, moccasins, wampum belts, and a beaded sash and baldric (shoulder strap). Much like the Angolan slave's jacket, the baldric combines English cloth with native design: the strap is dark blue wool with a red strip around the edge and contains scroll elements composed of alternating stripes of the red fabric and white glass beads.[53] These curving forms have a long history in southeastern native decoration, having been found on late prehistoric ceramics of the Lower Mississippi.[54] They appear on virtually every surface created or embellished by southeastern Indians and suggest the coiled, sinuous energy of snakes, animals that appear frequently in Cherokee myth and that were associated with life-giving water and powerful crystals.[55]

The baldric scroll design thus shares with the Angolan slave attire an indigenous potency that transforms trade cloth into something individual and communicative. While no specific narrative adheres to either item of dress, the slave coat and Native American baldric both convey vitality and index agency. The description of the Angolan man's clothing demonstrates that more than 250 years ago, a black slave used indigo to craft a design that visually announced his identity.

Further, the baldric tells its viewers that at about the same time, an Indian lifted onto a shoulder a strap of indigo-dyed wool enlivened with turning spiral forms that visualize life energy in abstract but suggestive form. With these two items, blue-dyed Negro cloth and Indian blue duffel are transmuted from featureless fabric into adornment that connected their wearers to cultures that survived, transformed, and flourished in colonial South Carolina.

PART 2

Indigo Cultivation and Production in South Carolina

CHAPTER 3 ❧ Botanists, Merchants, and Planters in South Carolina
Investments in Indigo

BRITISH SETTLERS IN SOUTH CAROLINA initially experimented with growing indigo not long after the colony's founding in 1670. The settlers were hoping to find agricultural ventures that would become as successful as the sugar plantations of the British Caribbean, and they tried the dye plant alongside other crops because blue dye had a ready market in Britain. However, settlers could not immediately commit wholly to indigo or other export crops but first had to concentrate their energies on finding subsistence and protection from hostile Indian and Spanish neighbors.[1] When colonizers began planting in earnest in 1690, rice proved well worth the required investment of time and resources, since it flourished along South Carolina's waterways and was heavily consumed abroad. However, rice fortunes declined at the beginning of the War of Jenkins's Ear in 1739, leading to indigo's reintroduction in South Carolina. The conflict with Spain caused shipping costs to spike, largely because of increases in insurance rates. Rice, a bulky commodity, became expensive to transport, whereas indigo dye was sold in light, compact cakes. Moreover, because indigo could grow on rice plantations' dry soil, its growth complemented rice cultivation. Britain encouraged South Carolina planters to commit to indigo by offering a bounty on it. Under these conditions, indigo helped secure planters' fortunes through the Revolutionary War.[2] During this period, thousands of pounds of South Carolina indigo made their way to England: at the trade's 1775 peak, just over 1,122,000 pounds of indigo were exported.[3] Indigo literally and figuratively became the business of botanists, merchants, and planters. Those who studied the plant acquired intellectual capital in the form of admiration and acknowledgment from their peers. Growers and sellers of indigo gained patriotic pride as well as money, providing their nation with a key ingredient for manufacturing. And planters accrued cultural capital when indigo's cultivation was subsumed into pastoral writing that celebrated plantation life. These varied forms of indigo's value thread through and around the life of Alexander Garden, a Scottish physician, botanist, and planter who resided in Charles Town from the mid-eighteenth century until the Revolutionary War. Garden and his associates' involvement with the blue dye plant illustrates how intellectual, economic, patriotic, and cultural investments colored South Carolina Britons' commitment to indigo.

Botanizing and Indigo

Garden studied and invested in indigo while experiencing the intellectual and pecuniary rewards of the plant world. The Charles Town–based physician, for whom the gardenia was named, was a significant contributor to the development of natural science, specifically botany, and was well known among other natural scientists across the British Atlantic. Garden collected local knowledge; formulated understandings of southeastern plant, animal, and mineral specimens; and shared much of this information with fellow enthusiasts, including natural historian Carl Linnaeus, members of the Royal Society in London (Britain's premier organization devoted to science), and amateurs throughout the British colonies. Although he emigrated from Edinburgh to Charles Town in 1752 as a physician and worked hard at that profession, treating colonists and their slaves during his tenure in South Carolina, Garden's true calling was botany, and he wished he could devote himself exclusively to it. His preference for examining and learning about plants is evident in his many letters to natural scientists, and although he was pleased to live in a place that offered the opportunity to discover things that no Briton or European had yet encountered, he was equally distressed to be far from important metropolitan centers of learning and the many knowledgeable men who inhabited them.[4] Garden's profession and calling coincided when he learned of plants that caused or cured illness, but he did not focus on studying these synergies. Instead, his pursuits were divided among medicine and botanizing (discovering and classifying plants).[5] His wide range of experiments to determine the useful properties of plants did not focus exclusively or even predominantly on their medicinal properties. Although he was driven in part by curiosity, Garden was motivated more by his determination to become a respected member of the elite brotherhood of British and European virtuosi, those who saw themselves as responsible for gathering and systematizing knowledge of the world's natural resources. Therefore, Garden assiduously applied himself to assist Linnaeus in his project of recording and naming all flora that came to his attention, worked hard on papers that he hoped the Royal Society would publish, and lobbied to participate in botanizing missions in the Southeast.[6]

In 1756, Garden corresponded with a vice president of the British Royal Society of Arts (RSA), an organization that had been established two years earlier to promote the arts, including the cultivation of plants for knowledge acquisition and use. The RSA wanted Garden to develop one of several American branches of the society, which sought to persuade colonial planters to try new crops and thereby raise Britain's already high international standing in the intersecting realms of science and commerce. Garden eagerly agreed to take on the task. He published a notice about the venture in the *South Carolina Gazette*, seeking planters with whom he could work. The following year, Garden told the RSA that South Carolina planters were reluctant to involve themselves in cultivation experiments unless they were guaranteed a return on their investments that equaled what they obtained from indigo.[7] Although this economic calculus frustrated the botanist in Garden, he came to understand it well when he became a planter who experimented with indigo and a British Loyalist during the Revolutionary War who tried to fund a voyage to England with the dye.

Garden became interested in indigo not long after moving to Charles Town and studied both how the plant was grown and how dye was made from it, describing the two procedures in letters to colleagues.[8] He became well acquainted with Eliza Lucas Pinckney, who loved the vegetable world as much as Garden did, and the two discussed her successful experiments with indigo ten years earlier. Thus intrigued with dye plants, he conducted his own experiments with a plant associated with red dye, the prickly pear. In 1757, Garden sent the Royal Society his findings about this cactus, information he framed in relation to his understanding of indigo. The cochineal insect harvested for red dye feeds on the prickly pear, and Garden reasoned that if the red obtained from the beetle originated in the cactus, cultivators could harvest it rather than the insect, which is difficult to pluck. To test his hypothesis, he fed the cactus to two children and a nursing slave, checking the urine of the former and the milk of the latter for signs of red.

He reported that he found the color in both substances and noted that his idea for the experiment came from an earlier observation that cows produce blue milk after eating indigo plants.[9]

Garden's intellectual investment in indigo—suffused by the excitement of discovery, the importance of use value, and the lure of recognition by fellow enthusiasts[10]—also colors the 1760s and 1770s natural history expeditions of Garden's acquaintances, John Bartram and his son, William. The Bartrams visited an indigo plantation not far from Charles Town, and William made a brief but significant foray into indigo growing.

John Bartram had an established, productive farm with a well-known garden on the Schuylkill River in Pennsylvania and became the most respected collector of colonial natural specimens for British and European natural historians, surpassing Garden.[11] Bartram's botanizing was supported by English wool merchant and natural history enthusiast Peter Collinson, who had Bartram named royal botanist to George III (a position envied by Garden and other natural historians). This appointment enabled Bartram to travel through southeastern lands such as East Florida, territory acquired by England from Spain in 1763, at the end of the Seven Years' War, a British victory that virtually ended Spanish and French threats to Britain's power in continental America. William Bartram, an ineffectual merchant with a penchant and talent for natural history drawing, also made the journey, greatly deepening his appreciation of nature and motivating him to make another expedition to the area years later. Father and son began their adventure in 1765 with a trip to Charles Town, where they discussed botanizing with Garden, visited prominent merchant and planter Henry Laurens's city home and gardens, and traveled with Garden and Laurens to outlying plantations, most notably that of John Deas, where indigo flourished alongside corn in an experimental double planting. Back in town, the Bartrams made the acquaintance of John Stuart, recently appointed Indian commissioner for the southern region, who joined Garden and Laurens in aiding the Bartrams during their sojourn in East Florida.[12]

The three South Carolinians helped John Bartram set William up as an indigo and rice planter along the St. Johns River in Britain's new colony. Perhaps taken with Deas's magnificent establishment in South Carolina, certainly captivated by East Florida's natural wonders, and sure of their own understanding of the vegetable world, the Bartrams felt that William stood an excellent chance of growing good indigo and rice and relied on the expertise of their Charles Town–based friends to provision the younger Bartram. In 1766, the two men returned to South Carolina, where Laurens advised them on what to acquire for a plantation. Laurens facilitated their purchases, including slaves, whom Garden examined to certify their health.[13]

Although William Bartram was an inept planter, doing as poorly in this venture as in his others, the miserable conditions to which he sank—observed and duly reported by Laurens[14]—did not tarnish his love of East Florida's land, people, and flora and fauna. After subsequent business mishaps in Pennsylvania and elsewhere, he convinced his father's new patron, Royal Society member John Fothergill, to fund another journey to the Southeast, which William planned to document with an illustrated travelogue. During this 1773–77 trip (ultimately curtailed by the Revolutionary War), William Bartram conveyed his fascination with and respect for the environment and people he encountered through text and pictures, and he deemed many of the places he visited ideal for indigo cultivation.[15] Although he may have been chagrined by his personal failure with indigo and he certainly valued his labor as a natural history artist over his business activities, Bartram continued to view much of what he experienced through its use value. Unlike his father's published account of their earlier journey, which reads mainly as a promotional tract for settlement,[16] William Bartram's travelogue is infinitely more concerned with vivid description as a marker of his engaged and artistic intellect. However, with its references to potential rich indigo lands,[17] William Bartram's work demonstrates that an investment in scientific capital could easily slide into visions of monetary capital. Indeed, indigo equally fired the pecuniary interests of Garden's and the Bartrams' peers who were committed to seeing Britain's colonial plantation enterprises dominate world markets.

Nationalistic and Financial Commitments to Indigo

The Bartrams' work demonstrates not only how commercial interests thread through eighteenth-century botanizing and the lure of its intellectual cachet but also how these intertwined impulses were informed by nationalistic concerns. John and William Bartram's publications functioned in varying but important measures as promotional literature for British investment in plantations in East Florida.[18] Indigo was the staple most often pursued as a "guaranteed" success for those who planted in the new British colony,[19] and this enthusiasm was based on South Carolina's indigo boom, which had freed Britain from dependence on France or Spain for the dye.

Earlier forms of promotional literature had been instrumental in encouraging South Carolinians to invest in indigo to improve both their personal circumstances and those of the empire.[20] Two notable contributors to a stream of publications on why and how to plant indigo in the colony were merchant James Crokatt and dye inspector Moses Lindo. Crokatt was the first to author a major treatise on indigo growing in South Carolina. Lindo was a champion of the plant and its dye in South Carolina throughout the staple's mid-1750s–mid-1770s success in the colony. Although neither indigo booster wrote with the authority of a natural historian, as the Bartrams subsequently did, Lindo was something of an amateur botanist, having published in newspapers the knowledge he acquired of dye and medicinal plants.[21] Lindo and Crokatt really established themselves in the London and Charles Town marketplaces, where they carved out significant roles in the world of commerce while broadcasting the importance of indigo to a mother country that wished to free itself of any reliance on its rivals.

During the 1720s and 1730s, when trade in rice dominated a market that also featured the export of deerskins acquired from Indians as well as naval stores and foodstuffs produced by settlers, Crokatt was an important merchant in South Carolina. He moved to London in 1737 to specialize in South Carolina trade, and his business boomed.[22] Because indigo was light to ship and had a good value-to-weight ratio, Crokatt saw that the planters and merchants in the colonies had much to gain from committing to indigo, provided the quality of their dye rivaled that of French- and Spanish-produced dye. In two treatises on indigo published in 1746 and 1747, Crokatt instructed South Carolina planters on the best approaches to cultivating indigo and making dye from it, knowledge that he gleaned from other sources and supplemented with advice from master gardener Philip Miller of London's esteemed Chelsea Physic Garden. Crokatt also added details about shipping methods and costs, along with particulars about how the dye was graded and priced in London.[23] In every instance that pertained to growth, production, evaluation, and use, Crokatt referred to successful methods employed by the French and Spanish, encouraging South Carolinians to employ the same means to guarantee the good reception of their product. He warned that shoddy manufacture would prevent South Carolina indigo growers from succeeding.[24] Although his language was not jingoistic, he argued that in addition to enriching themselves through the making of fine indigo, South Carolina planters would benefit the homeland.

> I wish some method were thought on to have an account kept of all [indigo] made in Carolina, and shipped off last year and this; so as it might be sent to London, and laid before the proper officers, as the introduction of an application to parliament for a duty to be laid on French, and a bounty granted on, British plantation made indigo; . . . it would make a difference . . . to the Carolina planters; and I am persuaded will be granted for seven years, providing the province agent is instructed to apply for the same; and that it should appear probable you can make what's needful for the use of Great-Britain, which I think is not to be doubted.[25]

Indeed, Crokatt subsequently helped to obtain the bounty on South Carolina indigo about which he had speculated.

Lindo published several assessments of the colonial dye in widely read newspapers, pointedly asserting that South Carolina indigo was in a position to eclipse its rivals. Lindo, a London dye inspector, came to South Carolina shortly after indigo cultivation began there and proclaimed his intention to benefit both the colony and Britain by building up South Carolina indigo's reputation.[26] Although some contemporaries found his efforts exclusively self-serving, Lindo continually averred that he was most interested in helping secure quality colonial blue dye for Britain: "I flatter myself the world will be satisfied of my integrity of heart and the uprightness of my intentions; as well as be convinced, that I have devoted myself to the service of my native country, and equally so to this province."[27] Whatever his motives, Lindo's rhetoric illustrates how nationalism girded economics of the period and suggests that even if planters created personal wealth through indigo, they could take equal pride in having provided British manufacturers with a key staple. In defending South Carolina indigo, Lindo put his considerable reputation on the line.

That self-interest and national pride had equal shares in South Carolina indigo production is also evident in Garden's writing—specifically in his meditations on planters' overriding concerns. In a series of letters written between 1759 and 1773 to John Ellis, a merchant and Royal Society member, Garden pointed to the bottom line in the calculus of personal enrichment versus experiment for the mother country. Ellis and other British natural historians wanted Garden to oversee the planting of a provincial garden in Charles Town, with the idea that it would serve as a sort of horticultural lab for experiments with foreign seeds. Ellis and his colleagues were eager to find more "green gold" for Britain by discovering plant commodities that could grow well in the colonies. In the debates about creating a Charles Town–based unit of the RSA, Garden had argued that planters likely would not want to devote time and resources to growing experiments that might fail to provide them with the yield they obtained from indigo. The same set of concerns seems to have undermined plans for the provincial garden: although Garden supported the project and put considerable effort into realizing it, it failed to get off the ground.[28] South Carolina's agricultural enterprises clearly would succeed only when national gain was accompanied by personal gain.

Personal Fortunes and Indigo

Garden's friend, Henry Laurens, perfectly exemplified such meshed interests. He was an American patriot during the Revolutionary War but prior to the conflict had been deeply embedded in and proud of his business with London. Laurens had become one of South Carolina's wealthiest men by providing Britain with essential staples—among them indigo—from the colonies. Sent from South Carolina to London in the mid-1740s to learn trade from Crokatt, Laurens returned to Charles Town in 1749, becoming a successful merchant. By 1755, he had built a stately home in the colonial city's East Bay suburbs and hired a gardener from England to create one of the colony's finest living collections of exotic plants.[29] The income that fed Laurens's commercial empire derived from a business model that was highly synergistic. He imported slaves to drive South Carolina's plantations and exported staples grown on his and others' plantations. Laurens then set about establishing further agricultural ventures, first in the low country and subsequently in Georgia, the South Carolina backcountry, and East Florida (where he primarily supported enterprises run by other people).[30] Laurens's first foray into planting was a joint venture with his brother-in-law, John Coming Ball: in 1756, the two bought a plantation in St. James Santee Parish, where they grew rice and some corn. In 1762, Laurens became sole owner of Mepkin, a plantation well situated for land and water transport to Charles Town, thirty miles away. This property was not only a country residence for his family but also the site where he practiced agricultural diversification. Mepkin produced prodigious amounts of firewood as well as lumber, corn, rice, and indigo. From 1766 to 1773, the dye plant provided 11 percent of Laurens's total commodity sales from the plantation, and from 1765 to 1769, Mepkin was devoted almost solely to indigo after Laurens (incorrectly) predicted that prices for the staple would surge.[31] Indigo remained an important element of Laurens's diversified business enterprises. As a merchant, he sold indigo grown by himself and others, and he grew the crop on acreage in the Ninety Six District and at Mount Tacitus, a large indigo plantation on the Upper Santee River that he purchased in 1777.[32]

By that time, war had erupted with England, and although the conflict ultimately ended South Carolina's indigo boom—independence cost the colony its primary purchaser of blue dye—indigo remained a key guarantor of wealth into the later 1770s and beyond and as such a means of security in difficult times. This is evident in the entwined dealings of Garden with his close friends, Charles and George Ogilvie, an uncle and nephew who collaborated in mercantile and planting endeavors.

Indigo as Security

Charles Ogilvie had befriended Garden, a fellow Scot, in Charles Town. When Ogilvie set off in 1761 to establish himself in London, he had letters of introduction from Garden and had promised to act as the latter's agent there. Garden, in turn, helped look after his friend's plantations, Richfield and Mount Alexander.[33] In 1764, George Ogilvie entered his uncle's London business, which sold indigo, among other goods, and the younger Ogilvie subsequently contracted with his uncle to develop family land in South Carolina, including his cousins' plantations, Myrtle Grove and Belmont.[34] In 1773, at Charles's request, George paid Garden's Royal Society admission fees when the botanist won election to the august body, a gift that firmly linked George to his uncle and to Garden.[35] George arrived in South Carolina shortly thereafter, and Garden took the young man under his wing, providing him with a comfortable home when he took a break from managing his far-flung and barely inhabitable family properties.[36] This place of respite was Otranto, the rice plantation Garden had bought in 1771 on Goose Creek in St. James Parish. Not far from John Deas's indigo tracts, which Garden had visited with Laurens and the Bartrams six years earlier, Otranto was the site of Garden's work with indigo. He experimented with seeds from China, eager to determine how these plants differed from and perhaps improved on the indigo already grown in the colony.[37]

Although Ogilvie ordered his slaves to plant and cultivate primarily rice at his uncle's and cousins' properties,[38] indigo served as a source of economic security for the young planter as well as for Garden in the wartime years of the later 1770s. Both men used the commodity to finance moves to England: Ogilvie had to leave because he refused to take an oath of loyalty to the colonies, and Garden planned to depart because his health was failing and he believed that it would improve in England and because he correctly feared that he would be branded a Loyalist. Garden first attempted to finance his departure in 1777 by investing in thirteen casks of indigo, which were lost at sea; he tried again the following year, attempting to transfer capital in the form of indigo to England, but the ship carrying it was taken by a privateer.[39] Through Garden, George Ogilvie also used indigo to attempt a new start in England. On the young man's behalf, Garden traded slaves and some stock from Charles Ogilvie's Belmont Plantation for eight thousand pounds of indigo, giving George a cask to convey with him on his journey home.[40] At about the same time, Garden also worked to provide economic security for his family: he placed his properties, including Otranto, as well as forty-two slaves, livestock, furnishings, and other goods in trust for his wife and children.[41] Although Ogilvie and Garden lost the bulk of their wealth during the war, indigo as capital was a key bulwark in their defense of their estates.

The loss of these estates not only constituted a huge blow to both men's finances but drained them of their pride as planters. Planting entailed a sense of cultural identity, enabling those who grew staples for Britain to see themselves as proper English gentlemen firmly embedded in the pastoral tradition. Indeed, Garden attached himself to this realm when he purchased Otranto, and Ogilvie dramatized the image of the plantation as a patrician villa in a poetic hymn to the botanist's estate. Indigo subtly but markedly colored such cultural investments for a number of South Carolinians.

Indigo and the Pastoral Tradition

During much of the eighteenth century, Britons embraced neoclassicism, framing their cultural pursuits and shaping their surroundings in relation to their understanding of Greek and Roman civilizations. These endeavors were often shaped by a Greco-Roman-inflected and idealized husbandry through which patrician cultivators beautified land by making it productive. This phenomenon is most clearly visible in the stately city and country homes erected by Laurens and other planters and featuring arbors, gardens, and sometimes Greco-Roman follies inspired by neoclassical British estates.[42] British pastoral sensibilities also held sway in Georgic writing of the time, including "didactic agricultural poetry," which "attain[ed] a considerable degree of popularity."[43] Several key publications in this genre, including a poem, championed indigo as a crop, reflecting Britons' commitment to pastoral sensibilities. Indeed, such sentiments infuse the rhetoric of the advice on indigo planting published by lawyer and planter Charles Pinckney in a 1744 issue of the *South Carolina Gazette*. Further, pastoral language and form overtly determine the structure of an anonymous 1757 poem on indigo, likely the work of planter Charles Woodmason, that also appeared in the colonial newspaper.[44]

Pinckney penned several influential essays on indigo cultivation under the pseudonym Agricola, and his choice of moniker points to his as well as his readers' commitment to the discourse of antiquity. Other contributors to the gazette who wrote about indigo also took up Roman-style names such as Agricultor and Mercator.[45] In the tone of an enlightened patrician, Pinckney reported on experiments with the dye plant by his wife, Eliza Lucas Pinckney, and imparted the expertise gleaned from her efforts. He also shared accounts by authorities on indigo, including excerpts from Philip Miller's *Gardeners Dictionary*, information from a manuscript by a South Carolina indigo planter from the previous century, and specifics obtained from French prisoners of war.[46] The service that Pinckney and others with Roman pen names who published on indigo planting provided their contemporaries not only echoes botanists' spirit of collective engagement but also recalls the image of civic-minded Romans bent on improving the circumstances of their community.

This viewpoint structures the 1757 poem on indigo, written to whet an appetite for a collection of verse to which the author hoped readers would subscribe.[47] Woodmason, the poem's likely author, had acquired experience growing indigo, as is evidenced by a 1755 piece he published in *Gentleman's Magazine* that included instructions for how to provision and run an indigo concern, including a detailed breakdown of costs and a woodcut showing dye works.[48] Perhaps eager to frame himself as a gentleman, Woodmason also wrote poetry,[49] a form of writing practiced and consumed by the gentry, who valued literary as well as practical arts. The *South Carolina Gazette* and other period publications reflected current interests in the practical art of agriculture and the aesthetic pleasure of poetry by printing hymns to cultivation modeled on verse by Hesiod and Virgil.[50] Woodmason's poem celebrates the indigo planter as a noble shaper of land who sagely responds to environmental conditions and wisely directs slave labor to improve the natural world, making it productive. The final third of the poem argues that the muse of Invention inspires the planter, who, like the Roman conqueror, avails himself of necessary and proper resources—slaves and land—to create ordered and beneficent property:

> All-conquering *Rome* to thee first owes her
> Birth,
> How universal is thy Pow'r on Earth!
> She peopled this new World, she still explores
> *Angola's* Coast, and savage *Gambia's*
> Shores,
> In Search of Slaves, a Race in Numbers
> great,
> Whose Constitutions, temper'd to the Heat
> By situation of their native Soil,
> Best bear the scorching Suns, and rustic
> Toil:
> But joyful Spring returns, the Winter's
> past,
> The trees bud forth nor dread the Northern
> Blast,
> Break off Delays, and thus p r e p a r e the
> Plain,
> Let Two Feet void 'twixt every Trench remain.
> Tho' some, imprudently, their Room confine,
> Allowing half that Space to every Line.
> Give Room, one Stem as much shall yield,
> And richer far the Weed: So shall thy Field
> With greater Ease from noxious Herbs be
> freed,
> And knotty Grass that choaks the tender
> Weed.
> So shall the Root by larger Banks be fed,

Nor fear the Rays from piercing Phoebus
shed.
Cautious of this, in Lines direct and true
(For Order's best, and pleases best the
View)
Extend thy long-stretch'd Furrows o'er the
Plain
Then invoking Heav'n for speedy Rain
Sprinkle the Seed, &c.[51]

That Charles Pinckney admired the poem is not surprising: the work must have resonated with his pastoral sensibilities and appealed to his civic interest in shared knowledge. One year after the verse was published, Pinckney, writing as Agricola, resubmitted it to the gazette, remarking that he had followed the directions for planting indigo in the poem and found them useful.[52]

Poetry, indigo planting, and a physical site of the pastoral converged at Garden's Otranto, which inspired George Ogilvie's 1776 Georgic ode to the plantation, *Carolina; or, The Planter.* The young Scot wrote poetry to take his mind off the dismal conditions that he experienced while overseeing the establishment of his cousins' plantations,[53] and Otranto, a perfect embodiment of the pastoral ideal, was the right place for him to experience and write about his dreams of intellectual, artistic, and botanic cultivation. Ogilvie celebrated his mentor's standing as a learned botanist by detailing virtually every plant that Garden cultivated on his property ("The smooth green meadow, or the enamel'd glade, / Where all the pride of Europe's florists yield,") and every book that his friend housed in his small Greco-Roman-style library:

A Temple, Sacred to each Muse, we find,
Where all the elegance of Art conspires
To grace the Authors ev'ry age admires.
Plac'd by their favour'd pupil's grateful hand,
In splendid rows, the healing Sages stand.[54]

The poem's vivid details, clothed in voluptuous language, paint a picture of a South Carolinian pastoral paradise owned by a studious gentleman, a possession available only to someone with financial savvy as well as strong ties to and pride in British culture. Although Ogilvie's meditation on Otranto does not feature indigo, Garden's writing about and experimentation with the plant are a key part of what enabled him to enjoy his stature as a natural scientist and gentleman planter. In Ogilvie's representation of Otranto, pride in the intellectual, nationalistic, economic, and cultural commitments that supported South Carolina's investments in indigo conjoin.

When Garden acquired his beloved Otranto, the property was known as Yeshoe.[55] Like many South Carolina place-names, that moniker was Indian. These textual and verbal traces of native presence are reminders that the lands cultivated by colonists such as Garden originally were inhabited by indigenous people.

CHAPTER 4 ❧ The Role of Indigo in Native-Colonist Struggles over Land and Goods

SOUTH CAROLINA'S GROWTH as a staple producer depended on Indian land and Indian goodwill, both of which were cemented with, as well as compromised by, trade. Indigo was infused into this mix when colonists began cultivating the dye plant on what had been or was still native land and Britain began using the dye to color cloth, some of which was exchanged with natives. When indigo became South Carolina's second staple, it assured and strengthened the colony's ties to agriculture along with Britain's ability to produce "homegrown" blue textiles to sell throughout its domain. South Carolina indigo was thus an important component in the exchanges of land and goods that drove colonists further into South Carolina's interior and placed blue cloth into native hands as a means of smoothing business and diplomatic transactions.

Prior to colonization, South Carolina was Indian Country populated by native peoples who had very different relationships to land and natural resources than did the British. While Indians identified themselves with land and cultivated it, they did not parcel it out through individual ownership or turn vast tracts of it over to introduced crops for export. These latter practices accompanied the British throughout their colonies, and they were tolerated by natives in South Carolina when Britons avoided land Indians considered off-limits and when the two sides concluded mutually beneficial agreements involving trade and protection from enemies. Indigo became part of this phenomenon in the middle of the eighteenth century and remained a component of the sociopolitical dealings among colonizers and Indians through the Revolutionary War.

An example of the links among settlement practices, indigo cultivation, and Indian strife appears in a mid-eighteenth-century letter to South Carolina governor James Glen. In 1756, the same year that Alexander Garden corresponded with the agriculture-boosting Royal Society of Arts about South Carolina indigo, Moses Thomson wrote to thank Glen for securing peace with neighboring Indians and for promoting indigo production: "I verily believe there was never such a firm Peace made with any Indians before and all advanceing the Manufactory of our Indigo and likewise your great Care of our back Inhabitants for when I was Major under your Excellency I cannot forget your Care by your Instructions to me several Times."[1] Thomson's missive shows that Glen helped propel indigo production into South Carolina's backcountry reaches. In fact, two years earlier, the commissary general who served under Glen "announced that he had six bushels of Guatemala [indigo] seed to distribute to the back settlers, a pint to each family."[2] This gift points not only to the success indigo had achieved as an export but also to the fact that South Carolina's commitment to staple agriculture entailed expansion into regions populated by natives.

However, the peaceful relations with Indians that Thomson believed Glen had forever assured were in fact intermittent: South Carolina's colonial history is shot through with multiple and complex Indian dealings shaped by intense struggles over territory and goods. Colonists wanted Indian land for agricultural pursuits along with native customers for manufactured wares; Indians wanted those items and sometimes South Carolinians as partners in battles with indigenous and foreign enemies. These goals were occasionally in synch, frequently at cross-purposes, and eventually contributed to disempowering South Carolina's original inhabitants and many other native peoples with whom South Carolina colonists came in contact.

Indigo's role in this dynamic is significant. By the time Thomson wrote to Glen, lands that eighteenth-century South Carolinians had acquired from Indians were planted with indigo, and blue garments and cloth that natives received from colonists were dyed with the same indigo. This spread of blue across Indian lands colors how Indian life was affected by colonization. South Carolinians' commitment to a planting culture and a concomitant Indian trade resulted in British and Indian exchanges of sites, goods, and services that rarely benefited native people. Indigo production contributed to these developments by entrenching colonists' investment in agriculture, playing a key part in backcountry settlement plans promoted to further and protect South Carolina's stakes in planting, and helping colonists maintain relations chiefly beneficial to themselves and often exploitative to natives.

Early British Colonists and Indians

Britain's first successful colony in South Carolina, started in 1670, gave rise to a series of settlement practices that were repeated largely unvaried throughout the course of the colony's growth as well as its differentiation into Georgia and Florida. First, colonists established themselves on Indian land to grow food and experiment with staples while commencing trade with natives for goods and services.[3] Second, colonists expanded across territory to increase trade and especially agriculture as well as to protect themselves from perceived threats. And third, colonists used land as a vehicle to buffer relations with Indians, in some key instances by giving Indians (ostensibly) inviolable reservations to ensure that natives would accept growing numbers of plantations. This tripartite matrix of British encroachment was overlaid on top of an earlier, massive disruption of native experience: disease introduced by initial European explorers and would-be colonists.[4] Foreign illness drastically altered native populations across the Southeast not only through pandemics but also via resulting social reorganization: after disease (as well as battles with white and native enemies) decimated their populations, various Indian groups merged to ensure their survival.[5] By 1670, when British colonists from Britain and Barbados created the first successful British outpost in South Carolina under proprietors given land for service to the Crown, tens of thousands of natives had perished. Among those who survived were the Catawbas, Cheraws, Cherokees, Chickasaws, Congarees, Creeks, Natchez, Peedees, Savannahs, Westoes, and Yamassees, who established smaller settlements and town complexes that stretched from the low country shore into the backcountry mountains.[6]

The remaining natives found their social instability compounded by the British colonists in their midst: the British settlers who founded Charles Town took tracts of land for planting and established trade relations with natives, and both developments fomented discord that resulted in Indian enslavement. Although colonists from Barbados brought African slaves to cultivate land—sugar growing had enriched many British Caribbean landholders, and plantation culture was a model to which South Carolina settlers aspired—planters wanted more labor as well as "resources" to export. They therefore began traffic in human chattel with Indians who captured and sold their indigenous enemies.[7] Natives performed another service for colonists by hunting deer: "Between 1699 and 1715, the colony annually exported an average of nearly 54,000 deerskins to England. In later years, annual totals sometimes exceeded 150,000."[8] The animals' skins were popular in England for making breeches and gloves, and in exchange for these hides, Indians acquired many items they found useful, most notably dress items as well as guns, which aided their pursuit of both slaves and deer.

Indian trade initially overshadowed the colonists' planting concerns:[9] although colonists had slaves, the work necessary to clear and establish agricultural land on all but a subsistence level required time. The British in and around Charles Town experimented with staple crops, including indigo, to see what might flourish in South Carolina. However, more than twenty years of these experiments, enormous amounts of hard slave labor, and substantial engineering projects were required to make low country waterways produce rice, the colony's first winning staple. As plantation enterprises picked up, growers acquired more Indian land by fanning out up and down the coast, and colonists unable to invest in large-scale agriculture also encroached on Indian territory by moving further inland to conduct business with natives.[10] For a time, Indian trade stayed ahead of plantation building, although as rice production rose steadily, the grain joined deer hides as a major export. During the 1720s, "rice production tripled to more than 16 million pounds."[11]

While planting and Indian trade often existed synergistically—especially because a number of merchants were stakeholders in both businesses—colonial traders with Indians were sometimes accused of practices that undermined the colony, including its focus on agriculture. Such charges dated back to South Carolina's time as a young colony battling some native peoples as well as French and Spanish colonists (especially at St. Augustine in Florida), all of whom felt threatened by British expansion in the Southeast. Hostilities resulted in raids that took South Carolinians further into Indian territory, and the ensuing volatile relationships with Indians escalated slaving. Infuriated Yamassees and their allies, including the Catawbas and Creeks, ultimately attempted to drive South Carolinians from the region, nearly succeeding during the 1715–17 Yamassee War. The natives killed many colonists, beginning with traders, and destroyed numerous properties, including multiple plantations.[12]

The loss of these plantations contributed to colonial policies that restricted Indian trade when powerful government officials who were also planters held

Indian traders responsible for the destruction Charles Town and its environs suffered.[13] Planter legislators understood that trade was a key to positive relations with natives: if Indians were happy with goods they received, they not only provided the colony with valued commodities but also helped protect South Carolinians from their enemies. However, these politicians equally understood that trade could produce dire consequences if it was conducted in ways that alienated natives. And unregulated trade had done just that, encouraging cheating, permitting alcohol sales to Indians that provoked disorderly conduct, and compounding slaving and thus inciting further violence while dismembering native communities.[14] Charles Town politicians had attempted to right matters in 1707 by creating an assembly-appointed board of commissioners to liberate wrongly enslaved Indians, forgive Indian debt incurred through unscrupulous trade, establish an Indian agent to ensure the proper conduct of business, and license traders.[15] Nevertheless, trade had continued largely unchanged by these efforts, despite natives' complaints. Only after the huge losses of the Yamassee War did the South Carolina assembly put some (temporary) teeth into Indian trade regulation: a 1716 law outlawed private dealings with natives and stipulated that all such commerce had to be conducted on behalf of the colony in forts at Savannah Town, the Congarees, and Wineau.[16] By making trade a government rather than private affair, legislators diminished traders' power and pecuniary interests.[17]

Politicians were able to take these steps because traders' destabilization of the Indian experience was more visible than similar fractures wrought by planters; however, colonial agriculture subsequently joined trade as a clear menace to Indians, a turn of events powered not only by the colony's expanding rice cultivation but also by its investment in indigo. An event that foreshadowed agriculture's impact on Indians occurred in the wake of the assembly's 1707 attempts to control Indian trade. That year, South Carolina set aside a tract of land on the southern edge of its border for the Yamassees (forfeited when the Indians turned against the colony), not solely as a bulwark against the Spanish but also to ensure that the natives did not begrudge the expansion of South Carolinian plantations.[18] The colonial government created other such Indian reservations in the coming years—notably for the Catawbas, Natchez, and Peedees—but only the Catawba reservation survived agricultural development to exist (in shrunken form) into the present day.[19]

Indigo and Settlement on Indian Land

Britons in the young South Carolina colony wanted better protection and more advantageous rights to land than the proprietors were able or willing to provide, and the fate of the Yamassee reservation after South Carolinians' near defeat by the natives provides a good example of why the colonists wanted to throw off the proprietors. Hoping to defend their colony against hostile Spaniards and Indians, the South Carolina assembly earmarked the territory for a buffer settlement of small farms; then, to ensure their own pecuniary gain, the proprietors sold the land to a Scottish baronet.[20] In 1719, aggrieved colonists successfully petitioned the Crown to assume control of South Carolina. British officials understood the colony's value both as weapon against Spanish and French ambition in the Americas and as a staple producer. Britain's investment in South Carolina as a plantation region proved wise, for rice exports boomed from the 1720s to the early 1740s.[21] When rice profits slipped for a time because of the increased shipping costs and privateering that came with war, indigo's success demonstrated that the colony could still be counted on to produce "green gold" for the home country.

Indigo was also a key investment for South Carolina residents, providing not only planters with a crop that could grow on rice plantations and help make up for losses incurred from falling rice profits but also yeoman farmers with a staple to produce beyond the tidal region. In addition, indigo gave colonial legislators a strategy for encouraging backcountry settlement to allay fears about threatening populations. Beginning around 1720, rice cultivation had driven up land prices in the coastal zone and along nearby waterways and propelled an influx of African slaves for labor.[22] Blacks outnumbered whites in the colony by more than two to one, and officials feared slave uprisings.[23] In 1730, to encourage more white settlement through farming, South Carolina's governor, Robert Johnson, set up a township scheme that awarded fifty acres for each member of a household (including slaves) in regions chosen for their strategic worth as bulwarks against Spanish, French, and Indian enemies.[24] In part conceptually similar to the South Carolina assembly's plans for the Yamassee reservation, under which frontier farmers would be the first defense against enemies, the township project also mirrored many South Carolinians' vision for the Georgia colony, which had been established in 1732: a barrier of small-scale farms that would hold at bay hostile Spaniards and Indians.[25]

The township plan was also viewed as a means of securing access to and protecting transit networks long used by Indians that connected the backcountry and low country, rivers and Indian paths prized as vehicles for bringing crops to Charles Town and taking manufactured goods to settlers and native trading partners.[26] Township sites set aside for small farming ventures were therefore carved out of areas in which Indians were firmly established, places where native trade was already being conducted and that in some cases already had forts or Indian trading posts. Williamsburg was set up alongside the Black River; Fredericksburg was on the Wateree River; Amelia, Saxe-Gotha, and Orangeburg were sited between the Congaree and Santee Rivers; and Long Cane was situated between an offshoot of the Savannah River (where New Windsor was located) and the Saluda River. Further, the Catawba Path cut through Fredericksburg; Amelia, Saxe-Gotha, and Orangeburg were established to protect the major Indian path that ran from the Piedmont to the coast; New Windsor was next to Fort Moore, which was created as a defense against the Cherokees and Creeks and where Indian trade was conducted; and Long Cane (which the Cherokee claimed as their land) was near Ninety Six, where Robert Goudy had an Indian trading post.[27]

Some backcountry townships were sited on land that Indians had already cultivated, priming it for development. Smart land investors appear to have sought out areas that natives favored for growing corn, squash, and beans. In 1737, John Thompson purchased for three hundred buckskins land from the Cheraw and Peedee Indians along the Peedee River.[28] In addition to part of the Cheraw Path,[29] his acquired acreage had "old fields" (native farmland) that became a draw for a group of Welshmen who wanted to set themselves up along the Peedee. Two years later, Thompson appeared before the South Carolina Council to prove his ownership of the land the Welsh wanted; the council then purchased it from Thompson and assigned it to the interested Britons. The so-called Welsh Tract contained about forty old fields that the colonists went on to till.[30] Thus, backcountry farming was facilitated not only by the land and water trade pathways that natives had established but also by Indians' cultivation of fields. When indigo planting subsequently boomed, at least one Welsh Tract family raised it: Robert Williams and his son, David, "prosper[ed] by making indigo and raising swine."[31]

Whether colonists acquired primed or "wild" land beyond South Carolina's coastal region, indigo was a wise investment, offering "more inducements to the frontiersman than any other money crop." The dye was inexpensive to transport to Charles Town, and the plant "grew readily in either middle or back country soil."[32] Unlike rice, which required wetlands that scarcely appeared beyond the tidal zone, indigo could be established on varied terrain and complemented other crops with which incoming settlers had experience. In 1754, when indigo was presented to colonists headed for the backcountry, farmers who already knew how to plant staples such as wheat and flax were pouring into South Carolina from the mid-Atlantic region and Upper South, driven in part by native unrest stirred up by the French precisely to cause a British colonial exodus. These newcomers were joined by immigrants from Europe, drawn not only by the belief that South Carolina homesites would be free from Indian attack but also because of the incentives offered by the colony's government, and the backcountry became one of British North America's fastest-growing agricultural regions.[33] By the mid-1760s, indigo was a significant part of mixed-crop farming practices, and certain places, especially in the Peedee area and below the fall line in the middle regions of settlement, became known as particularly hospitable for the plant.[34] Household records, notices, and personal papers show that very small as well as larger indigo-growing establishments sent the dye from the backcountry to Charles Town for shipment to England.[35] Those significantly involved with indigo included Alexander Burnside, who had 250 pounds of indigo in an inventory from his Catawba River property; merchant and Indian trader Joseph Kershaw, who had indigo works on his large Camden plantation and sold indigo seed at his store; and Moses Kirkland, who owned a 950-acre indigo plantation in the Ninety Six District. These and other men who worked with indigo on a larger scale sometimes collaborated with small indigo growers (who also joined forces with one another at times) to maximize production and processing of the dye plant: some exclusively produced seed, while others made their indigo works available to those who lacked such facilities.[36] Backcountry indigo cultivation was also further maximized with slave labor: while yeoman farmers personally contributed to the staple's growth, larger planting concerns in the area required bound labor. Indeed, in 1772, the bulk of slaves sold in South Carolina were sent beyond the tidal zone: as low country planter Peter Manigault informed merchant-planter Henry Laurens, two-thirds of slaves were purchased by settlers in the backcountry, where planters were regularly obtaining "150 wt of indigo to a hand."[37]

Further Destabilization of Colonist–Indian Relations

The 1750s and 1760s were characterized not only by successful backcountry indigo production but also by major backcountry conflict between Indians and colonists. This unrest occurred in the frontier regions of South Carolina and Georgia (which grew when its prohibition against slavery was lifted in 1750) as well as in East Florida after 1763, with strife fueled by unchecked greed among Indian traders and settlers. The 1750s brought to the southeastern backcountry farmers as well as large numbers of Indian traders and merchants who worked to supply natives along with the white newcomers. This major influx of colonists not only dispossessed natives of land but increased the amount of hunting in the area, which, in turn, lowered the number of deerskins natives could acquire for trade. An overabundance of traders also created a surfeit of durable goods, allowing unscrupulous traders, now free of the rigid restrictions, which had long since expired, to sell rum as well as manufactured wares to Indians and to accept stolen horses as payment from natives who had no deer hides.[38] Although Indian slaving was no longer big business since natives had been decimated by disease and surviving Indians came to resist a trade that further compromised their numbers, many natives found themselves beholden to traders who had allowed them to incur massive debt.

Because Indian land and trade were key to South Carolina's growth and defense, savvy midcentury colonial politicians built on earlier efforts to keep natives satisfied with their white neighbors, although these attempts trailed off as the balance of power came to favor colonists. Dealings with the Peedees, Natchez, and Catawbas provide examples of the economic and diplomatic calculus that linked land, goods, and protection to ultimate native disempowerment. In a repeat of the effort to situate the Yamassees on reservations and in part to facilitate colonial expansion, South Carolina in 1738 gave the Peedees and Natchez one hundred acres of land for one thousand years in the region of Four Holes Swamp, a tributary of the Edisto River.[39] In 1763, the colonial government also established a fifteen-square-mile reservation for the Catawbas along the river that bore their name, near the border with North Carolina.[40] In the intervening quarter century, these native groups looked to the colonial government to settle disputes with other Indians as well as with colonists, and goods—particularly dress items—featured in the events that followed. In 1744, some Catawbas traveled to Charles Town to report the killing of some tribe members by Natchez forces; the Catawbas were persuaded not to retaliate by government presents that included cloth.[41] In 1753, the widow of the Peedees' King Robin, a headman murdered by "the Northern Indians," was mollified by the colonial government with a gift of fabric from the bursar.[42] In the 1760s, the Catawbas' King Heigler declared himself "white" (perhaps drawing on Indian symbolism in which the color signifies peace) and repeatedly committed his warriors to the colony, specifically because South Carolina clothed his people.[43] Nevertheless, in this instance, Catawba complaints about colonists' encroachment on the reservation fell on deaf ears. South Carolina had just defeated the powerful Cherokees, who battled the colony from 1758 to 1761 over trade and land abuses, and politicians must have felt that the weaker Catawbas posed no threat and that the colony consequently had nothing to gain by appeasing them.

The events that led up to and shaped the Anglo-Cherokee War provide another case of how linked trade and land negotiations disempowered natives. By 1730, the Cherokees were firmly enmeshed in relations with colonial South Carolinians; although they did not yet covet the natives' backcountry territory, colonists traded with the Indians and involved them in protecting plantation interests. That year, South Carolina arranged with Cherokee headmen to provide their people who captured runaway slaves with guns and clothing.[44] Like the Peedees and Catawbas, the Cherokees and other southeastern natives, including the Cherokees' traditional enemies, the Creeks, had come to depend on British guns, clothing, and tools. These goods did not supplant native traditions but instead improved on them: for example, guns made killing game and foes easier, while manufactured garments and cloth made for ready dress. Indians not only found these material objects both useful and satisfying but believed that they physically instantiated ties to Britons by making visible their mutual commitments to provide for and protect each other. Indeed, while visiting London in 1730 to affirm ties with Britain, Cherokee leaders Attakullakulla,

Usteneca, Ouconnastotah, and accompanying warriors took pains to drive home this point.[45] South Carolinians who failed to understand the emblematic value natives attached to goods were frustrated with Indians' expectations for gifts, and at various points in the colony's history, officials attempted to cut funding for Indian diplomacy.[46] The Cherokees were insulted by such actions as well as others that cheapened their agreements with South Carolina, especially trade arrangements and land negotiations that benefited colonists at the Indians' expense. By midcentury, the Cherokees were angry that their Creek enemies secured better payment for their deerskins,[47] that traders frequently were unscrupulous, and that South Carolinians eyed Cherokee homelands. When settlers began establishing farmsteads in Cherokee Country and some tribal leaders were killed after trade relations disintegrated, the Indians launched a war that terrified colonists. Although the first British campaign against the natives was a disaster, the second, led by James Grant, routed the Cherokees.[48] Grant and his men, including Henry Laurens, razed Cherokee towns and laid waste to the Indians' extensive agricultural lands, and because those natives who survived had little food, the Cherokees surrendered.

Subsequent peace negotiations, meant to stabilize Indian relations, centered on Cherokees' demands for a ready supply of goods—primarily clothing—and guarantees regarding the inviolability of their lands. That indigo-dyed material played an important role in addressing the former is evident in 1762 advertisements for Indian trade items published by the South Carolina Directors of the Cherokee Trade: blue strouds were at the top of their November 19 call for goods.[49] Duffels also featured prominently in other such requests, and since "blew Duffields for Match-coats" appeared on virtually every period trade list for the Creeks,[50] it is a fair assumption that many duffels destined for the Cherokees were blue as well. However, although the Cherokees had more access to cloth and other wares after ceasing hostilities with the British, their lot was not secure. After 1763 accords, virtually anyone could get a license for trade, which was thus largely unregulated,[51] and South Carolinians failed to respect the boundaries established for Indian Country, settling wherever they chose. Although British cloth and clothing prized by natives passed into Indian hands around this time, the immediate satisfactions these items provided weighed little against the losses sustained by Cherokees and other southeastern natives. Ironically, South Carolina indigo showed up on native bodies during this period in large part because the dye plant spread further and further into Indian territory, cementing indigo's place as a prize staple that served the British textile industry.

This dynamic played out further for the Cherokees as well as the Creeks in events that shaped Georgia's development. The influx of settlers that had begun in the 1750s mushroomed after 1763, when the Seven Years' War ended and Britain received possession of East Florida. Along with yeoman farmers, British investors with plantation interests as well as Indian traders saw great opportunities in the South Carolina–Georgia–Florida nexus of established transportation routes, exchange relationships, and new territory. Although the traders and planters who set themselves up in one or more of the three regions at times ended up in competitive and problematic relationships with one another, these tensions paled compared to the disruptions natives faced as a consequence of white encroachment. British plantations pushed natives from their traditional homesites, and British settlers, whether large- or small-scale farmers or merchant-traders, overhunted deer. Creek and other Indian trade partners stole horses to pay for rum, which supplanted oversupplied durable goods in trade exchanges and to which natives became addicted.[52] Although long-term South Carolina and Georgia traders established in and around Augusta blamed the ensuing unrest on newer traders, the former were complicit in a scheme to have natives settle their debts by giving up land.[53] Merchant-traders with successful planting ventures had shown new settlers that profits could be maximized when land was involved. Alexander Garden's good friend, George Ogilvie, who conducted business in South Carolina and England, made money not only in exchanges among colonists, London merchants, and natives but also from his plantations.[54] And when Henry Laurens and other South Carolinians with agricultural experience turned much of the coastal region between the Savannah and Altamaha Rivers into plantation frontier in the early 1760s, a period when several reports on indigo as an ideal crop were published, further expansion into regions beyond those good for rice was assured.[55] Indeed, indigo became the chief staple produced in East Florida and an excellent investment for Georgians: surveyor William De Brahm declared in 1772 "that a Georgia indigo farm could earn more than the 29 percent annual profit that a new rice plantation paid back to an investor."[56]

The wheels were put into motion to displace Indians on a huge scale in 1767, when merchants, traders, landed interests, and government concerns all began to see the gains that could be achieved by taking over a large swath of native territory for planting. Wealthy merchants, including London-based John Nutt, who invested heavily in Indian trade, wrote to the Board of Trade arguing that Britain would benefit economically by establishing more North American colonies in backcountry regions and proposed doing so by securing Indian land.[57] Colonial stakeholders in London as well as Georgia saw how to realize the value of this plan in 1771, when colonial traders cut a deal in which they agreed to absolve the Cherokees of their debt in exchange for a sixty-square-mile tract on the Savannah River.[58] Although this arrangement enraged the Creeks, who laid claim to the area in question, as well as Indian affairs superintendent John Stuart, who disapproved of colonial versus royal arrangements with natives, Georgia governor James Wright made good on the agreement by acting as a British representative with colonists' interests at heart. Indian traders won Wright's support by emphasizing in a letter to the governor that the land was ideal for several crops, with indigo heading the list:

> This tract contains upwards of three millions of acres of as fine Lands & as fit for the Culture of Indigo, Tobacco, Hemp, Flax, Wheat & other valueable produce as any in America, having the advantage . . . That the lands to the Norward, are much Worn out, & very Insufficient for the increase of Population in those parts, as appears by the Number of emigrants that flock from thence into the upper parts of So. Carolina & Georgia, where they are obliged to remain, being unable thro poverty to transport their Familys by Water to the Floridas, and prevented them from Journeying by Land by several Nations of Indians they have to pass thro.[59]

The resulting 1773 New Purchase, enacted through the Treaty of Augusta, saw 2.5 million acres pass from the Cherokees and Creeks (who participated because of promised gifts and an agreement that trade would occur in specific locales) to the Georgia colony. Although virtually all involved were dissatisfied with how the New Purchase was realized—deals with Indians were broken, and Wright brokered land sales that upset merchant ambitions[60]—the arrangement demonstrates how almost a century of unequal colonial and Indian partnerships that turned on land and trade culminated in extreme losses for natives.

Foreshadowing these events, South Carolina's first Indian agent, Thomas Nairne, had dreamed in 1708 that Britain would acquire vast tracts of Indian land to fuel colonial agriculture. Traveling with an Indian trader to native settlements as far as the Mississippi, he penned an enthusiastic letter to the British secretary of state, Lord Sunderland, outlining a plan whereby Britain could expand to the Gulf of Mexico to counter French colonization. Nairne envisioned conquering the Southeast for his native country by building a vast plantation network on the ruined towns of Indians who resisted domination and with the slave labor of recalcitrant natives as well as that of Africans.[61] By the New Purchase, much of what Nairne imagined had in fact come to pass, first in South Carolina and subsequently in Georgia and East Florida: Indian territory was turned into plantations and farms on which slaves labored. The spread of colonial agriculture that transformed Indian Country occurred in tandem with colonial trade. Dependent on British cloth, among other wares, to secure their well-being and to cement diplomatic relations, natives lost ground in trade exchanges: they literally forfeited land when they could not pay for goods obtained from traders. South Carolina indigo was not only the crop that paved the way for agricultural expansion beyond South Carolina's coastal region but also the dye that tinted much of the British cloth that Indians acquired. The plant and the colorant therefore visibly marked—indeed powerfully indexed—struggles over land and goods in colonial South Carolina and its environs.

CHAPTER 5 ❧ Producing South Carolina Indigo
Colonial Planters and the Skilled Labor of Slaves

IN 1779, GODIN GUERARD of Prince William Parish placed a notice about a runaway slave in the *South Carolina and American General Gazette*. As was common for such notices, this one included detailed information about the runaway so that readers could identify him. Guerard sought Jupiter, a young man between twenty-four and twenty-five years of age who had been born in South Carolina and who stood five feet, four inches tall. The planter stated that he had bought Jupiter from Gabriel Manigault of Silk Hope Plantation, where the slave's relations lived; this information would have led readers to infer that the runaway would likely return to the plantation or its vicinity. Guerard further noted that Jupiter had few but large front teeth, a "complexion as yellow as that of an Indian," and "short Negro hair" and that he had left with a "homespun jacket," a "half-worn duffil blanket," and "osnabrugs trousers (indigo-died)."[1] This advertisement shows that slaves who grew indigo and made dye from it were Indian as well as African. The South Carolina–born Jupiter was a "mustee" slave: part Indian and part African. His clothing refers to his heritage and station: Indians typically wore duffel blankets as matchcoats; Indians as well as Africans wore osnaburg (an inexpensive type of linen); and slaves were often outfitted with homespun and were sometimes able to enhance their clothing with indigo dye.[2]

Most South Carolina plantation narratives fail to account for the Indian slaves in the midst of the thousands of enslaved Africans who toiled hard to produce indigo and other staples that rewarded many white colonial men with intellectual, financial, and cultural capital. Native slaves comprised a quarter of the colony's slave population in 1708,[3] and although their numbers later paled beside those of African slaves—imported in large numbers as rice planting came to dominate South Carolina's economy—they are still evident in late colonial and early federal records.[4] Indian slaves began as one of South Carolina's first exports and remained a component of the colony's commercial enterprises throughout its history: they labored in homes and on properties in every position that black slaves occupied, including jobs relating to indigo production.[5] Further, natives intermarried with African slaves and, like their black counterparts, bore white planters' children. Indeed, although the practice of Indian slaving slowed and disappeared after the middle of the eighteenth century, Indians remained embedded within the fabric of South Carolina's slave culture past the colonial period.[6]

Like black slaves, bound Indian men and women lost not only their homelands but also their freedom to South Carolina's slave-based agriculture. South Carolina indigo culture gained from the skilled work of enslaved people, who added important expertise to a set of processes that ensured the staple's success in South Carolina. Moreover, these skilled slaves were supported by others whose contributions in and out of the home made plantations and farming ventures thrive.

Bound Labor for Profit in the Atlantic Economy

Slaving in the American Southeast and in Africa shared some important features: Britons acquired slaves from British slavers and indigenous people of both regions in exchange for manufactured goods, particularly guns and cloth. This trade practice encouraged warfare, disrupted power relations, altered economies, devastated communities, and forever changed the people and places that survived slaving. In the seventeenth and eighteenth centuries, millions of Africans were torn from their homelands by British slavers and sent via factories on the Slave Coast—from the Bight of Biafra to the Bight of Benin—to Caribbean and North American plantations to produce staples for food, building, and manufacturing.[7] In the same period, thousands of Southeastern American Indians were exported to Caribbean plantations, sent north to labor in Britain's American colonies, or kept closer to home for South Carolina and other southern planters' use.[8] African and Indian slaves were commodities, became the property of those who bought them, and produced the raw materials that comprised Britain's manufactured goods, which were consumed throughout its empire. African and Indian slaves thus both instantiated and created wealth for others and did so in South Carolina in part by making indigo.

When colonists from Britain and Barbados established Charles Town, they had black slaves in their midst; however, rather than obtain more Africans, they initially enlarged their small bound workforce through Indian slaving. The proprietors subsequently forbade the practice to avoid alienating natives, whom the British hoped would support the colony. The colonists nevertheless continued to use animosity among indigenous populations to their advantage: they traded goods and promised military aid to Indians in exchange for captured enemies. South Carolinians sent these natives to the Caribbean as slaves, thereby obtaining a ready export commodity while ridding the colony of likely antagonists.[9] The settlers justified slaving to the proprietors by maintaining that individuals captured by natives were often subjected to death by slow torture, a disingenuous argument given the brutal nature of Caribbean plantation work and the widespread violence that slaving produced.[10] Although in the short term indigenous people such as the Westoes, Savannahs, and Yamassees accrued desired goods and trounced hated enemies through slaving, they rather quickly became grist for the mill: colonists consumed these tribes' people along with their territory.[11] And as natives became slaves retained by South Carolinians to work plantations on Indian homelands, indigenous people saw that colonists' slavery was completely unlike the institution within native cultures. Captives kept by natives were either adopted to replace dead loved ones or worked as community outsiders to help maintain homes and agricultural fields. Although the latter were not always well treated, they were not subject to the violent abuse experienced by many slaves owned by colonists: torture was not a gruesome, ongoing punishment for natives but was instead a death sentence to avenge kin killed by enemies.[12] As Indians allied with South Carolina fell victim to the dire consequences of colonial slavery, they fought back. Although the retaliatory 1715–17 Yamassee War almost destroyed South Carolina, the colonists prevailed, and while rebuilding their colony into the next decade, they acquired even more native slaves. However, Indian slaving fell off after midcentury, when colonists began to perceive African slaves as a better and less encumbered resource. Colonists' relations with Indians then stabilized into trade patterns that favored deerskins and ultimately land for British goods and services.[13]

From the beginning of the eighteenth century, African slaves greatly outnumbered not only enslaved Indians but free whites in South Carolina: indeed, as early as the 1670s, slaves comprised somewhere between a quarter and a third of the colony's population.[14] When colonists moved beyond mere subsistence concerns and turned their attention to staple production, the success of labor-intensive rice cultivation necessitated a very large workforce. The Caribbean sugar plantation model fueled by black slaves was replicated on the wetland plantations that developed around Charles Town, and as rice boomed, thousands of Africans were imported into the colony. Although more expensive than Indians, some Africans already possessed rice expertise that contributed to successful cultivation of the staple.[15] Moreover, a seemingly endless supply of Africans existed, they lacked their own sovereign communities to harbor them if they escaped in the New World, and they were free of political entanglements. The 1740 South Carolina Slave Code suggested just how sticky Indian slavery could be when it exempted from its draconian measures "Indians in amity with this government," terminology that in subsequent years enabled some natives to extract themselves from slavery.[16] Africans had no such opportunity, and their appearance literally colored their relationship to the colony. An Indian's complexion did not automatically communicate slave standing; an African's could.

Although South Carolina's Native American slave population was soon eclipsed by the African slave population, the two peoples were not only fellow chattel who worked alongside one another but regularly produced mixed-blood "mustee" offspring.[17] Often called "yellow," as in the description of the runaway Jupiter, these children were the living bonds that united red and black slaves.[18] A great many colonial initiatives sought to keep Africans and Indians separate and hostile—natives were paid to catch runaway blacks, colonial Indian traders were not supposed to use African labor, and black slaves were encouraged to report Indians sighted on colonist properties[19]—but the structure of colonial agricultural life produced circumstances that consistently and deeply allied natives and Africans. For example, the Alexander Wood family, deep in the midst of Goose Creek culture, the Barbadian-rooted plantation establishment near Charles Town, was supported not only by the labor of black slaves but also by that of enslaved Indians, mustees, and "half-breeds," children of Indian slave women likely fathered by the white patriarch.[20] Africans and natives were even more profoundly linked through Indian trader George Galphin, a major player in the nexus of trade and farming around Augusta at Silver Bluff. There Galphin fathered half-breed slaves, and possessed many African and mulatto slaves who worked the land he owned in Creek Country. Intermarriage occurred between some of these slaves: one of Galphin's black slaves, David George, who lived for a time among the Creeks, married another of his master's slaves whose brother was a mustee.[21] Indeed, Galphin's trade and planting concern, run by black and mixed-blood slaves (left to his sons by a Creek woman when he died), became one of the most important interracial sites of exchange in colonial South Carolina.[22] Although Indian, mustee, and half-breed slaves did not dominate the colony's bound labor force, their existence cannot be denied, and it testifies to the way in which indigo production truly drew from all populations.

Slave Labor in Accounts of Indigo Production

Whatever success South Carolina planters had in raising indigo and making dye was made possible by the work of slaves, not only directly but also indirectly, as they performed all of the labor that enabled plantations to run: building and repairing homes and outbuildings; keeping spaces clean and people fed, clothed, and healthy; fishing, hunting, animal husbandry, and gardening that put food on the table; packing and transportation of goods to market. White planters, overseers, and dye makers certainly learned from doing, but their expertise came chiefly from observation rather than from the repeated and strenuous bodily efforts that indigo production demanded.

White authors' written knowledge obtained by observing indigo making and by gathering others' understanding and experience with the plant is no more intrinsically valuable than slaves' know-how obtained from immediate interaction with the material conditions of cultivating and processing indigo. Nevertheless, texts about planters' involvement with the dye plant dominate today's literature on the staple, in part because these ledgers, letters, articles, pamphlets, books, and other documents have been archived and published, while slave knowledge has not been nearly as well preserved. Further, these texts provide detailed information about conditions and processes that is easy to obtain merely from reading. In short, planters' writings offer accessible, useful data that describe the efforts of all individuals working with indigo.

Indigo grew better in the Caribbean and Florida, where the weather was warmer and the soil richer, than in South Carolina, and the process of making dye was tricky.[23] Information about and experience with indigo production were consequently critical to the endeavor's success in South Carolina. As James

Crokatt's and Charles Pinckney's writings about indigo production make clear, planters who tried growing the crop drew on existing knowledge about it from publications (predominantly those by French producers in the Caribbean but including one by an early South Carolina grower) as well as tested their own hypotheses about indigo's growth and manufacture. Pinckney's future wife, Eliza Lucas, made indigo through trial-and-error experimentation, with shared experience from a neighbor planter, and with know-how sold to her father by dye makers from Montserrat, a British Caribbean island that had exported the blue dye to England in the early eighteenth century. Crokatt's and Pinckney's texts contained information gleaned from Philip Miller, head of the Chelsea Physic Garden, who in turn had relied on French Dominican Jean Baptiste Labat, who carefully described early eighteenth-century indigo manufacturing on Martinique.[24] Labat's observations replicated in Britons' publications provided specific information about when and how to plant, nurture, harvest, and make dye from indigo.

A treatise written by Elias Monnereau translated from French and published in London in 1769 demonstrates just how exhaustive such information could be. In *The Complete Indigo-Maker, Containing an Accurate Account of the Indigo Plant; Its Description, Culture, Preparation, and Manufacture with Œconomical Rules and Necessary Directions for a Planter How to Manage a Plantation, and Employ His Negroes to the Best Advantage*, Monnereau carefully expounds on all of these topics. Though specific to Caribbean conditions, the text addresses realities that also applied to South Carolina planters. Monnereau provided specific details for management of planters' property, a category that included not only land but also slaves. The volume also contains step-by-step directions for preparing soil, planting seed, weeding, insect control, harvesting, and dye making. In addition, Monnereau offered thorough instructions for overseeing slaves, detailing slaves' supposed indolent and devious natures and suggesting how to address their faults without crossing the line into brutality:

> I have just hinted at the rigour that it is necessary to observe with regard to the negroes; but care should be taken that it does not degenerate into cruelty, which is already but too frequent in our islands, where, upon a simple suspicion or a slight fault, unwarrantable cruelties are exercised. The chastisement should always be proportioned to the crime; if atrocious, it should not be spared; but small faults should often be winked at, otherwise punishments would be incessant.[25]

Although Monnereau's text conveys to some degree the mental and physical energies slaves brought to indigo growing and dye making—and certainly communicates the bodily pain slaves experienced if punished for misbehavior—he offers no insight into how indigo manufacture was indebted to African expertise.

However, other published accounts establish that in the seventeenth-century Caribbean, European and British labor organization practices combined with indigenous African indigo-making skills. In Barbados, British colonizers adopted the Spanish model in which indigo workshops were run by slaves, some of whom were observed employing dye-making procedures adapted from African practices. These slaves used hollowed-out logs to soak plants before pounding them with pestles in mortars, a technique of African origin.[26] Further, when British and European merchants in the Caribbean introduced South Indian methods of indigo production, which involved the use of multiple vats and an extensive beating process, the resulting economies of scale required wood paddles and on some plantations wood vats. Fabricating this equipment required substantial woodworking skills, which many slaves had obtained in their homelands.[27] Indigenous African knowledge thus found its way into Caribbean indigo-manufacturing processes that also included South Asian and European as well as British techniques and procedures. These amalgamated methods traveled to South Carolina with the first colonists from Barbados.[28] When Eliza Lucas helped to revive indigo production in South Carolina in the 1740s, her efforts were indebted to a Caribbean model of dye manufacture: dye makers from Montserrat provided her and her slaves with instructions on how the process worked.[29] It is also entirely possible that African indigo expertise was directly imported to South Carolina: many slaves brought to the colony during the indigo boom came from regions in Africa where indigo was cultivated and turned into dye.[30] Indeed, depressions called indigo pits on the grounds of a former indigo plantation on Edisto Island suggest this likelihood.[31] For centuries, Africans such as the Yoruba of Benin, the Manding of Mali, and the Hausa of Kano were renowned for indigo making and dyeing, with the latter employing pit vats to color cloth.[32] Although African blue dye is typically made by burning indigo plant material and pressing the ash into small balls, vat remnants can be an important dye ingredient.[33] African slaves may therefore have employed their native expertise with dye making and dyeing at an Edisto indigo concern.

More concrete information about slave knowledge of indigo making appears in illustrations from eighteenth-century publications, and one particular South Carolina artifact provides insight into the sustained, demanding, and expert work slaves' contributed to indigo culture. Careful study of indigo-making equipment and pictures that show slaves engaged with the plant enrich planter-created written documents. A set of indigo vats from Alexander Garden's Otranto plantation (rare extant eighteenth-century indigo vats),[34] along with several illustrations that show slaves at work with indigo, provide a clear and more human sense of slaves' indigo expertise as well as how indispensable their efforts with the dye plant were.[35]

Although the illustrations of indigo labor from M. de Beauvais Raseau's 1770 *L'Art de l'Indigotier*, as well as Henry Mouzon's roughly contemporary map of St. Stephen Parish, were not a source for South Carolina planters, they amplify written instructions with images of how slaves carried out the work. They therefore emphasize who did the hard labor of indigo making while suggesting just how demanding and skillful this work was. De Beauvais Raseau's illustration of planting indigo shows men either hoeing or plowing to prepare the ground and crouching women dropping seed (illus. 4). Slaves of both sexes are portrayed with visibly engaged muscles, bent backs, and bare feet. Small hills and trees dot the horizon, suggesting that the slaves are tilling and seeding a very large field, and because the slaves' bodies are arranged symmetrically and in synch with one another, the overall idea conveyed is that strenuous, repetitious labor was carried out over a lot of ground. Planter records note that more repeated small- and large-motor movement characterized crop maintenance, for slaves were responsible for plucking grasshoppers and other pests from indigo plants and weeding the ground around them.[36] The slaves' minimal attire in the de Beauvais Raseau illustration reminds viewers that heat, sometimes extreme, would have made the work even more difficult.

Although such strenuous physical labor is often not considered skilled and was not designated as such by eighteenth-century planters, the production of strong and healthy plants certainly required real understanding of the process as well as planning to minimize effort and discomfort. The symmetrical arrangement of figures and ground markings in de Beauvais Raseau's image produce a pleasing sense of order and mark the appropriate distance between plants for optimal growth; in addition, these features suggest that the slaves worked deftly in unison. The picture shows men and women coordinating their moves so that tasks smoothly follow each other, with unnecessary gestures eliminated as much as possible and energy consequently conserved. Although the illustration's symmetry is certainly in part the artist's conceit—a way of communicating order, control, and harmony at a plantation where forced labor could conceivably incite insurrection—it equally communicates slaves' skill at making demanding work easier to bear.

Mouzon's image of indigo harvesting and processing also emphasizes physical activity by contrasting bent-over slaves carrying cut indigo with the upright backs of the planter and overseer watching slaves toil (illus. 5). Here the distinction between the work of white and colored people is made explicit: the former observe (and perhaps guide) varied processes, while the latter perform the work. The labor is characterized as taxing (the human-size bundles of indigo stalks weigh the slaves down), demanding, deliberate, and repetitive. Both hard and lighter work are visually described in vignettes by the indigo vats. Three slaves maintain the water supply that runs in and out of the vats and ensure that weights keep the indigo under water. Although the slaves are not shown beating the fermented liquid that results from submerging the plant matter, the extremely long and thick paddles for this endeavor are propped nearby. The placement of the huge paddles suggests the effort involved in wielding them: they are set at a dynamic diagonal that points to the bowed slave backs. Beneath the paddles sit the trays for the indigo mud—the material that precipitates from the solution after oxygen is introduced by beating and an agent such as lime has been added—and to their upper right slaves cut dye cakes from the dried matter, stack them in a shed for further drying, and pack them in barrels for shipping. The individual producing the cut squares of dye looks female, and planter documents confirm that women did this work, which, like managing indigo in its liquid state, required a great deal of finesse. Henry Laurens greatly prized one of his female slaves, Hagar, for how well she tended his indigo paste, praising "her great care of Indigo in the Mud."[37]

Some of the equipment used in the final stages of indigo processing is documented in de Beauvais Raseau's illustration on the dye's manufacture: hanging bags for straining mud, trays and trowels for storing and smoothing it prior to cutting, and a large mortar and pestle—resembling those used to clean chaff from rice—for breaking indigo pods to collect seed (illus. 6). Two male slaves are shown crushing pods, and their tensed muscles and braced stances inject an impression of indigo production's physicality into a largely didactic representation of tools. The necessary coordination of their efforts suggests a regular rhythm, and the sense of repeated, deliberate movement is echoed in the tray of cut indigo mud bearing numerous, equal partitions. Precision and physical processes are thereby conjoined to communicate dexterity and know-how. Taken together, de Beauvais Raseau's and Mouzon's illustrations resolutely put laboring slave bodies into white writers' texts that describe indigo making, and these images reveal that the work was not merely demanding but also skilled.

These conditions can be readily inferred from studying the indigo vats from Otranto (illus. 7). Although it is not clear whether they were Garden's vats (preservation consultants date the vats to sometime between 1760 and 1800),[38] their composition and scale indicate that they were a challenge to build and to use. Long, tall, and constructed out of brick set and sealed with plaster, the vats are the product of a master mason's design and several construction workers' efforts. Fitted with sluices to drain water from one tank to the next and subsequently outside the works, the vats required not only a clear understanding of dye-making procedures but also sophisticated engineering. South Carolina's white planters, overseers, and dye makers would have acquired the knowledge necessary to create such vats from experienced indigo makers in the Caribbean but would not have built the vats themselves, instead tasking black bondsmen with the labor. Since the Otranto indigo works were produced after the staple was well established in the colony, slaves had enough experience with indigo and certainly with building to have designed and created the vats on their own.

In addition to building the dye works, slaves would have run them. Because the vats are big, slaves managing them would have expended a great deal of physical and mental energy. Filling the upper vat to submerge countless mounds of indigo stalks would have required substantial heavy lifting, and the workers would have had to evaluate a large amount of fermenting liquid to gauge how much lime the indigo required and how much oxygen had to be added via beating. Slaves also would have had to work paddles to agitate the indigo pool. During the course of this difficult work, they would have needed to examine carefully all dye residues that floated to the top of the liquid to decide when to drain the murky water.

Finally, removing the indigo mud from the bottom vat would have required time and careful handling.

The scale of the Otranto indigo works makes concrete another dimension of slave labor that is not visible in the vats themselves or in any illustrations of slave efforts. Planters' records and published complaints about indigo making in colonial periodicals make clear slaves' ability to excel in noisome circumstances. The chemical that produces indigo dye is the product of fermentation, and the quantity of dye produced at any given indigo concern was in direct proportion to the number of plants harvested and submerged in vats of water. The fermentation produces sickening odor, and large-scale works such as those from Otranto were therefore putrid places to labor. Slaves were not in a position to complain about the stink, as white neighbors did, and must have inured themselves to the stench and swarming flies attracted to decomposing matter to focus on the dye-making process.[39]

Despite the fact that written descriptions of work with indigo rarely provide human detail about slaves, and although the bodies pictured in the illustrations of indigo making are black, the runaway notice about Jupitor offers a good reminder that Indians were tied to indigo manufacture. An illustration from a 1773 map of South Carolina commissioned by the British Parliament demonstrates that colonists needed both Africans and Indians to support indigo production (illus. 8). The map represents an Indian alongside two white colonists, with an African slave hauling a container of indigo to a dock for shipping. The image's composition and the manner in which the figures are depicted suggest that the planters' and merchants' wealth and power stands at the center of and is propped up by the work of Africans and natives. The two colonists, positioned in the middle of the image, are shown in fine clothing, and one is pointing toward the scantily clad black slave off to the right, carting indigo on his bent back. The native is pictured at the far left, leaning slightly inward while seated on a rock amid plants that suggest South Carolina's natural terrain. He has a quiver of arrows on his back and is pointing a bow and arrow toward the other figures. The implied menace is contained by a tree stump that abuts the bow, and the Indian's hand appears slightly upturned, as if making an offering. Wearing a headdress and a mere blanket draped around his waist, he appears as "uncivilized" as the barely dressed slave: both are almost naked compared to the elaborately attired colonists. The Indian and African have curved shoulders and turn toward the white men, framing the colonists. These postures communicate the message that trade in staples such as indigo was built on the backs of hostile natives either kept at bay or enlisted as warrior allies and of Africans forced into slave labor. Although the Indian is not here represented as a slave, the two are made almost equivalent as props of white indigo planting and trade because of their shared positioning, near-naked state, and color.

That native slaves performed the same types of labor as their black fellows is evident in wills, inventories, runaway notices, and work advertisements that name slaves and describe the work they performed: William Robert Snell, who has produced the most extensive analysis of documents pertaining to Indian slaves in South Carolina, maintains that these individuals "were employed in most ways that Negro slaves were utilized."[40] More valuable slaves typically did specialized tasks that not only improved their owners' material circumstances but enabled masters to earn extra money by hiring out their chattel.[41] For women, such work consisted of all the activities that went into making and maintaining clothing as well as nursing (both the care of people and the feeding of babies); for men, it included all types of construction with wood, metal, stone, and brick; and for women as well as men it might entail cooking. Slaves listed in documents without a noted skill set often were field hands. Slaves labeled *Indian*, described as *mustee* or as having Indian features, and with names prefaced by *Indian* appear in documents of all types throughout the colonial period.[42] Laurens hired an Indian named Johnson who may have once been a slave or been born to slaves to run the East Florida indigo concern of a hugely wealthy associate.[43] Further, Indian and part-native slaves contributed to Eliza Lucas Pinckney's indigo plantation. The Pinckney Family Papers at the Library of Congress contain the names of the Lucas-Pinckney Indian and mustee slaves as well as enough information about one particular mulatto slave to demonstrate just how profoundly his labor guaranteed his owners' success with indigo. Indian land in tandem with Indian and African slaves made white low-country colonists such as the Pinckneys very rich, not infrequently by producing the blue dye that colored vast quantities of British cloth, including Jupitor's trousers.

Group of Negros, as imported to be sold for Slaves.

ILLUSTRATION I. William Blake, *Group of Negros, as Imported to Be Sold for Slaves,* from John Stedman, *Narrative of a Five-Year Expedition against the Revolted Negroes of Surinam, 1772–77* (London, 1796). Courtesy of the John Carter Brown Library, Brown University, Providence, R.I.

ILLUSTRATION 2. George Bickham, *The Three Cherokees Came over from the Head of the River Savanna to London*, *1762*. Courtesy of the Broadside Collection, Gilcrease Museum Archives, Tulsa, Okla.

ILLUSTRATION 3. [John Rose], *The Old Plantation*, Beaufort County, South Carolina, probably 1785–90. Courtesy of the Abby Aldrich Rockefeller Folk Art Museum, Colonial Williamsburg Foundation, Williamsburg, Va.

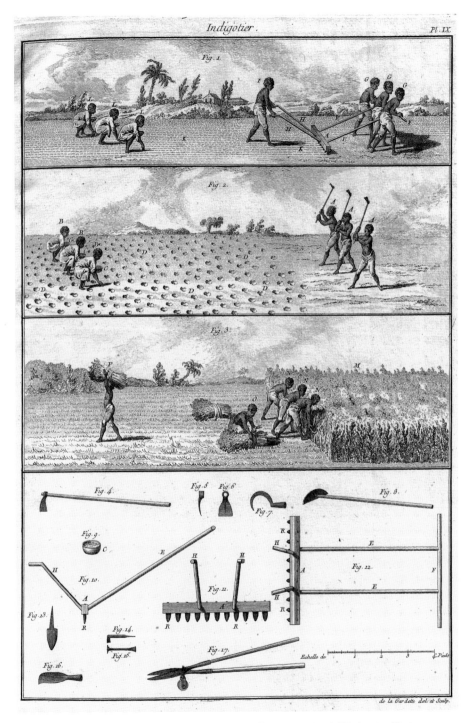

ILLUSTRATION 4. Illustration from M. de Beauvais Raseau, *L'Art de l'Indigotier* (Paris, 1770). Courtesy of the South Caroliniana Library, University of South Carolina, Columbia.

ILLUSTRATION 5. Illustration from Henry Mouzon Jr., *A Map of the Parish of St. Stephen, in Craven County* (London, 1773). Courtesy of the South Carolina Historical Society, Charleston.

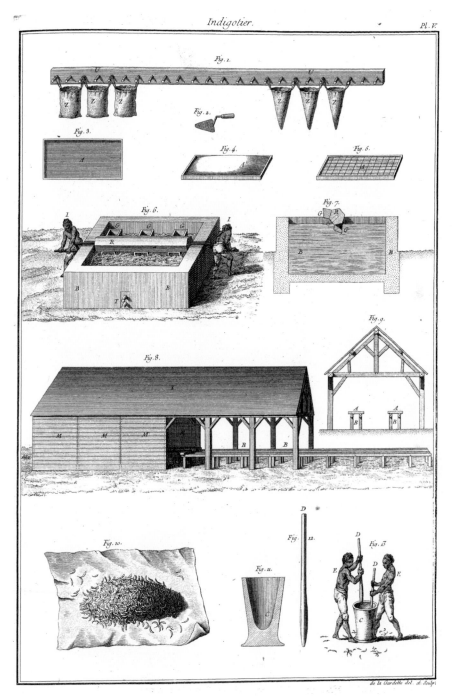

ILLUSTRATION 6. Illustration from M. de Beauvais Raseau, *L'Art de l'Indigotier* (Paris, 1770). Courtesy of the South Caroliniana Library, University of South Carolina, Columbia.

ILLUSTRATION 7. Otranto Plantation indigo vats, Goose Creek vicinity, Berkeley County, South Carolina. Courtesy of the National Park Service. Photo by David B. Schneider.

ILLUSTRATION 8. James Cook, *A Map of the Province of South Carolina* (1773). Courtesy of the David Rumsey Map Collection, www.davidrumsey.com.

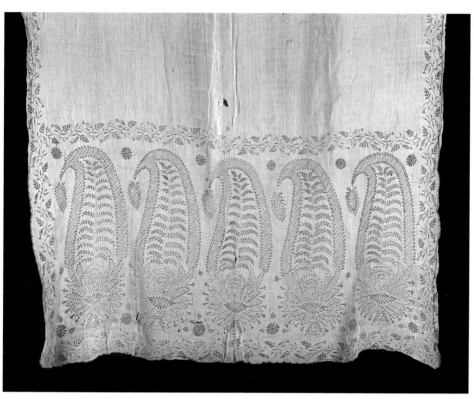

ILLUSTRATION 9. Woman's wrap with indigo plants design created by Eliza Lucas Pinckney, early 1750s. Courtesy of Tim Drake. Photo by Anderson Wrangle.

ILLUSTRATION 10. Reproduction of an eighteenth-century slave skirt created by Kendra Johnson and dyed with indigo, 2009. Photo by Anderson Wrangle.

PART 3

Indigo Plantation Histories

CHAPTER 6 ❧ Indigo and an East Florida Plantation
Overseer Indian Johnson Walks Away

ONE DAY IN 1767, "Indian Johnson," the overseer of a developing indigo plantation in East Florida, turned his back on the place he had managed well and
walked off into a swamp, never to be seen again. He left behind well-tilled fields,
at least fifty slaves along with a surplus of plantation-grown provisions to feed
them, and an extremely important absentee landowner and his surrogates in the
region, including the governor of East Florida.[1] Johnson's actions are difficult
to understand: he left a secure position working for and alongside some of the
most influential Britons in America, who were in a position to see that Johnson
was rewarded for his efforts. Moreover, he jeopardized his security as well as his
person by leaving the relative safety of the plantation for backcountry territory
that had only recently been won from Spanish enemies, was thinly settled by
Britons, and provided a former harbor for runaway slaves and a current sanctuary
for outlaws and potentially hostile Indians.

Johnson's departure from the indigo plantation he developed greatly frustrated
the man who had hired him, Henry Laurens. Laurens had not only cultivated
indigo in South Carolina's low country, where the plant was first successfully
grown in the colony, but also established it on his backcountry agricultural properties. Wary of East Florida's largely undeveloped land, limited infrastructure,
and small British population, Laurens decided against planting indigo or any
other crop there, but he did agree to help an important friend sink his many
resources into Britain's new colony. On behalf of Richard Oswald, a powerful slaver, merchant, and planter, Laurens worked with Oswald's silent partner,
James Grant, to establish the indigo concern that Johnson abandoned. Because
Oswald oversaw his commercial empire from abroad, he needed Laurens's and
Grant's help, relying on Grant, who settled in East Florida, to select the land

and manage lower-level appointments and on-site operations and on Laurens to supply provisions and staff the enterprise.[2] Although Laurens knew a great deal about running an indigo plantation and about the labor necessary to keep it going, he failed to find the right person to manage his friend's East Florida property. Johnson appears to have found little to gain by making a long-term commitment to Oswald's indigo venture. Indeed, Johnson must have gained by abandoning it, or he would not have done so. The important work that Johnson did—putting the plantation in order, provisioning it well, and readying it for productivity—laid a solid foundation for Oswald's enterprise on which subsequent overseers and supervisors built. Johnson's labors demonstrate that planters relied absolutely on their managers' ongoing on-the-ground efforts; his departure raises questions about how a native might make a place for himself in a land colored by indigo. Johnson's work was crucial for Oswald's success in a colony with conditions that Laurens rightly assessed as difficult. These conditions and Johnson's expertise worked to the Indian's personal advantage.

Laurens, Indians, and Indigo

Laurens possessed a range of experience with natives as well as with indigo, and the two realms converged in his dealings with Oswald. Before becoming a planter, Laurens was a leading Charles Town merchant, conducting business in a myriad of goods, notably deerskins acquired from Indians. Although Laurens is known for having accrued his formidable wealth through trade and subsequently by growing rice and indigo, he is less often presented as a merchant involved in Indian trade. Because he was the South Carolina–born child of a saddler, Laurens knew about the colony's native peoples and about the importance of the leather that Indians provided to British merchants. Therefore, the young Laurens quickly acquired expertise in deerskin trade.[3] He traveled to London, where he was apprenticed to James Crokatt, the preeminent South Carolina trader at the time, and dealt in the many deerskins that came from the colony to be manufactured into gloves and breeches. When Laurens went into business with other Charles Town merchants, deerskins remained an important export, and natives were key clients to be supplied with British goods. Laurens and his partners therefore did substantial business in Indian trade, even as Laurens established himself as a major dealer not only in rice and indigo but also in the slaves neces-sary to produce the two staples. Laurens's debt to Indian trade exemplifies a larger phenomenon: southern agriculture scholar Lewis Gray's work shows that profits from Indian trade built and sustained colonies until plantation culture was firmly established.[4] Philip M. Brown details how this dynamic played out in South Carolina, noting that between 1670 and the 1730s, various South Carolinians amassed wealth by trading with natives and then invested that money in rice and indigo plantations as well as farming ventures.[5]

When Laurens turned to planting, he embraced it fully: since he was based in the low country and had married into a planting family, he had ready access to the rice lands that were making many people rich and prominent. After he learned how to manage a plantation on his own—his first venture in rice growing was a joint enterprise with his brother-in-law—and discovered how to turn a profit producing crops, Laurens expanded his agricultural ventures with more land and more products, especially indigo.[6] His travels for business and as a soldier in the Anglo-Cherokee War took him to many parts of South Carolina, Georgia, and East Florida, giving him firsthand knowledge about the locations of the richest agricultural land. Thereafter, he bought swampy territory along rivers in South Carolina and Georgia for growing rice and invested in South Carolina back-country land for diversified agricultural pursuits. Because indigo complemented rice growing and mixed planting operations, it was a key constituent of his low country and backcountry concerns. And although he did not invest in East Florida—he worried that most settlers there were ill equipped to deal with its challenges—he supported not only Oswald's indigo-growing efforts but also the separate indigo project undertaken by Grant, who became the governor of British East Florida.[7] Laurens's involvement with these men was not mere goodwill: it enabled him to further expand his work with staples such as indigo. Through Oswald, Laurens partnered with two young merchants with planting ambitions, John Lewis Gervais and James Theodore Rossel, who scouted for prime land in backcountry South Carolina that Laurens could buy. They helped obtain acreage in Long Cane, an area that was claimed by both Cherokee and South Carolina colonists and that Laurens saw as an excellent spot for growing indigo.[8]

Long Cane was not the only part of Indian Country where Laurens acquired property: he was among the prescient South Carolinians who rushed to purchase land along the Altamaha River when Georgia received permission to sell that territory in the 1760s.[9] Natives in the region were greatly alarmed by these investors, correctly supposing that white settlers would quickly sweep up the entire area.[10] Laurens went on to establish what historian S. Max Edelman evocatively describes as a major rice labor camp along the Altamaha, with slaves toiling under grim conditions hacking Broughton Plantation out of the wilderness.[11] Laurens, however, made no record of trouble with Indians along the river. Indeed, even when Laurens noted Indian turmoil around Long Cane, he seemed certain that these disturbances would not affect his planting concerns there. Writing in 1763 and 1764, Laurens confidently maintained that the Cherokees who lived in the South Carolina backcountry were ultimately becoming hemmed in and immobilized by white settlers and that indigo would soon flourish in the area.[12] As Laurens predicted, the dye plant did well in several backcountry regions, and Laurens was equally happy that he could trade with natives and that they did not impede the growth of his plantation empire.[13] He was unhappy, however, when Johnson's departure from Oswald's East Florida indigo concern put his friend's enterprise in jeopardy. The Indian had worked hard to improve Oswald's estate, and his absence threatened the plantation's continued development.

Mount Oswald

Eighteenth-century British businessmen of Laurens's and Oswald's standing were not wont to place the success of their ventures in the hands of Indians. Although Indians might be significant trading partners in the colonial Southeast, they were just as often potential or real enemies who would not be entrusted with a powerful Briton's moneymaking ventures. Further, by the middle of the eighteenth century, white settlers in the Southeast feared uprisings by Native Americans and African slaves; Johnson's supervision of Oswald's human chattel stands in stark contrast to white initiatives such as runaway slave catching that pitted Indians and blacks against one another. It is therefore surprising that Johnson was trusted with the project of turning indigo into gold for one of Britain's elite.

Oswald's indigo-growing plantation, which Johnson managed for no more than a year, was part of a twenty-thousand-acre parcel, purchased by Oswald in

1765, that was well situated for growing and shipping staples. Grant had proposed the site to Oswald precisely for this reason: the estate, christened Mount Oswald, was located on the Tomoko and Halifax Rivers, forty-five miles south of St. Augustine, East Florida's key trading center and port.[14] Oswald carved his East Florida acreage into five settlements and had slaves plant indigo (at Grant's suggestion) as well as sugar. Oswald trusted Grant: he was a fellow Scot and a key military campaigner who knew the Southeast well, and as the governor of East Florida, he was intimately acquainted with the territory's conditions. Indeed, Grant was the prime mover behind Britain's attempt to turn East Florida into a staple-producing colony and championed indigo as the main crop for this ambitious enterprise. He became one of very few plantation owners who turned a major profit in East Florida, and he did so with indigo.[15]

Grant endorsed and took on indigo cultivation in East Florida because of the staple's success in nearby South Carolina, the economic calculus for its production, and East Florida's near-tropical climate, which was ideal for growing the dye plant and which yielded more than one cutting per season, more than doubling the output from a single planting. The crop neatly fit into an ambitious and imperial-minded planter's agenda in the American Southeast: it served Britain's mercantile interests and plantation owners' desire for large profits.

Oswald was such a planter: he had a huge and diversified business empire that stretched from Britain and its colonies to Africa. He was accustomed to using his many business contacts to help him hire on-site supervisors for his numerous enterprises,[16] and Laurens was a logical middleman to staff Oswald's East Florida venture. The two men had worked together in the slave trade, and Laurens's indigo-planting expertise and firsthand knowledge of East Florida meant that he was in an excellent position to select proper slaves and hire a good overseer for Mount Oswald. Well aware of the types of slaves necessary for indigo growing and dye making, Laurens advertised in the *South Carolina Gazette* for "two Negro Carpenters, two Coopers, three pair of Sawyers, forty Field Negroes, young men and women, some acquainted with indigo making, and all with the ordinary course of Plantation work in this Country."[17] On Oswald's behalf, Laurens purchased slaves that fitted these requirements as closely as possible and sent them to Grant, who found them well suited for plantation work in East Florida.[18] However, the first plantation manager Laurens selected, a white man named

Huey with solid experience, turned out to be a disaster. He proved lax, cruel, and untrustworthy, and he subsequently drowned, while Mount Oswald slaves looked on—and perhaps at their hands.[19] Laurens apparently had mixed feelings about his next hire for the position, Indian Johnson, and in light of the often difficult relations among Indians, blacks, and whites in the region, this choice seems especially curious. Laurens wrote to Grant that Johnson "must behave above the rank of common Carolina Fugitives, to save his Scalp a whole Year. He must be discreet and carry a steady command otherwise the Blacks will drown him too, for of all the Overseers they love those of their own colour least."[20]

The Color Line and Power Relations

These highly charged comments, which conflate fugitives, Indians, and blacks, speak volumes about how the color line and power relations were contested and negotiated in the colonial Southeast. Specifically, Laurens's remarks suggest that Johnson's actual or perceived ethnicity, in combination with his role as a plantation overseer, was an identity that he had to manage carefully at great risk. As a man who appeared to be part black, Johnson chanced being perceived as a potential traitor and killed by Oswald's enslaved blacks, especially if he treated them badly, as Huey had. Further, and more broadly, Laurens's reflection on Johnson's potential place within plantation power relations, together with the planter's observation that fugitives ran the risk of being scalped when caught, reveals that transgressors in the region were subject to swift justice meted out via the Indian practice of scalping.

Laurens's comments intimate that Johnson might have been taken to be a fugitive. In East Florida, fugitives had historically been South Carolina slaves seeking asylum among friendly Indians and free black communities or people of any color seeking refuge from the law in South Carolina or Georgia. During the fifteen years preceding Britain's acquisition of East Florida in 1763, at the end of the Seven Years' War, battles among Indians and white settlers encroaching on native lands bred extreme lawlessness in parts of the Southeast. In the tumultuous South Carolina backcountry, whites, blacks, and Indians stole from and killed one another, at times establishing mixed-raced bands of men associated with the Indian trade, hunting, and small-scale farming who stole property from wealthier settlers.[21] Therefore, by the time Mount Oswald was established, virtually any East Florida–bound man from South Carolina who was not of obvious high standing was seen as a potential fugitive—an escaped slave, an enemy Indian, a bandit of whatever color.

Laurens's scenario regarding what might happen to Johnson if he failed to exude propriety and authority at Mount Oswald reflects the tenuous hold of established hierarchies in colonial regions thinly settled by Britons, especially hierarchies shaped by color and ethnic difference. Indian attacks and slave rebellions in the North American Southeast—most notably South Carolina's 1715–17 Yamassee War and 1739 Stono Rebellion—had almost destroyed British towns and plantation complexes, requiring whites to expend great effort to protect their property, whether land usurped from natives or persons forcibly enslaved. Colonial politicians enacted treaties, passed legislation, and fostered policies that attempted to empower white gentlemen and their families and to keep them safe from hostile Native Americans and blacks. The power to treat and trade with Indians (some of whom were relegated to specific settlements) and to oversee slaves was officially entrusted to white men, although illegal trade and absentee planting meant that the situation on the ground was often far different, especially as British colonizers expanded in frontier regions in South Carolina, Georgia, and East Florida. The color line was especially unstable in these unpoliced areas, and white colonizers demonized or embraced Indians and Africans there depending on whether they were perceived as furthering or thwarting Britons' ambitions. In his missive to Grant, Laurens casts the hired overseer in both civilized and savage roles inflected by racial identifications. According to Laurens, if Johnson were to conduct himself like an English gentleman, he would succeed; otherwise, he would die like a savage at the hands of savages (meaning Indians or those who emulated their war trophy practices) or rebellious slaves.

Hiring Johnson

Despite Laurens's ambivalence about Johnson, the planter clearly had reason to think that the Native American could succeed where a white man had failed. Laurens had experience with Indians as cultivators and the opportunity to gauge their characters in cross-cultural undertakings, and in both sets of circumstances, he witnessed much that impressed him. Furthermore, he shared some of these experiences with Grant, which may have reinforced his willingness to take a chance with Johnson.

Laurens remained involved in Indian trade even after he diversified into other mercantile and planter activities. Although the number of deerskins that Laurens and other traders shipped to Britain declined over time, he imported into South Carolina increasing amounts of goods destined for Indian consumers.[22] Many of these goods were textiles, and from the 1750s on, some of the blue woolens that Indians favored were colored by indigo that Laurens and his associates produced in South Carolina and shipped to England.

Although Indian suppliers and consumers lay at the heart of the commercial enterprises that made Laurens rich, he had few direct dealings with Indians until he was drafted to serve as a lieutenant colonel in the Anglo-Cherokee War of 1758–61. This conflict also brought him into his first contact with Grant, the commander largely responsible for securing Britain's victory over the Cherokees. Grant routed the Indians by obliterating many of their towns and despoiling virtually all of their extensive agricultural lands, and Laurens participated in the decimation of the Cherokees' rich planting grounds. In a 1761 letter written from Indian Country, Laurens describes his feelings regarding this devastation: "We . . . plucked up at least 1,500 acres of corn, beans, melons, etc. This work, though necessary, often made my heart bleed. The Cherokees had totally abandoned these towns and fled with their wretched women and children across the mountains into the valley settlements. These have already suffered greatly and will be reduced to extreme misery as the winter advances."[23] This compassionate response stands in marked contrast to angry descriptions of supposed Cherokee perfidy in other Laurens missives about conflict with the natives—he bemoaned their "natural treachery & deceitfulness"[24]—so it cannot be said that he was at all times sensitive to Indians' circumstances. However, like Grant, Laurens regretted extreme measures taken against the Native Americans during the war, and both men faced public opprobrium when they argued against fellow soldiers and South Carolina politicians bent on revenge killings.[25]

Laurens and Grant knew that Indians could be great farmers, which explains the two men's willingness to employ Johnson as the overseer on Oswald's indigo plantation. Because Grant was in charge of and Laurens participated in the negotiations that ended South Carolina's hostilities with the Cherokees, the two colonists also had firsthand experience with Indian diplomacy and thus must have assumed that Johnson could handle the social and political challenges of serving as a plantation manager in the East Florida backcountry. Laurens spilled a great deal of ink in a heated public debate with his former friend, Christopher Gadsden, over the treatment of the Cherokees. Laurens expressed outrage at injustices committed against Indian peace delegates and noted their dignity in the face of abuse. In a long and detailed denunciation of Gadsden and his supporters, who argued vociferously for the scalps of Cherokee warriors thought to have killed colonists, Laurens described how Cherokee ambassadors stoically endured injury: "Notwithstanding many gross insults offered to them by us, since the Treaty of Peace was on the carpet, as for instance, personal affronts to the Ambassadors on their way down in several different places, and robbing them on their return, of their goods and horses, and one act of much more importance, . . . they have shut their eyes and their ears and would neither see nor hear them."[26] Although neither Laurens nor Grant can be described as an Indian lover, they certainly recognized Indians' strengths. Indeed, Laurens and Grant's shared experience during the Anglo-Cherokee War likely made them respect Native Americans' industry as farmers and integrity in the face of harsh circumstances.

Johnson's Expertise

Laurens's and Grant's knowledge of an Indian's potential to farm well, merit trust, and endure difficulties help explain why they came to have faith in Johnson as an overseer, a position with a great many responsibilities. The work of an overseer, while certainly not as onerous as slave labor, was hard in the best of circumstances and particularly challenging at a plantation such as Mount Oswald, which was in the early stages of development. Overseers were responsible for every aspect of a plantation's maintenance and output, since they were charged with caring for and protecting a planter's property and making it productive. Their duties involved supervising slaves' work (assigning and watching over their tasks as well as disciplining those who disobeyed); clothing and feeding slaves and nursing them when they were ill; ministering to livestock, tools, and grounds (including buildings and enclosures); and deciding when, where, and how to grow provisions.[27] Successful overseers thus had to strike a balance between stern authority and compassion as well as possess agricultural acumen, husbandry and building skills, and a degree of medical knowledge. In addition to these broad skills, Laurens must have expected Mount Oswald's overseer to possess knowledge about dye production, since his advertisement for slaves had sought those who were "acquainted with indigo making."

How and why Johnson obtained the skills that attracted Laurens's notice are unclear, although the history of Indian dispossession in South Carolina suggests some possibilities. By the time Laurens and Grant served in the Anglo-Cherokee War, most of the numerous Native American peoples who had inhabited South Carolina had been greatly reduced through introduced disease, warfare, and slaving. Only the Cherokees retained and populated their lands in South Carolina in relatively large numbers: the Catawbas had been pushed into smaller holdings, and the Creeks were located primarily in Georgia and subsequently East Florida. Dozens of other Indian peoples who lost land to British settlers merged into tribes that moved elsewhere or became what were known as Settlement Indians—that is, Native Americans in small communities that bordered white enclaves.[28] Other Indians—mostly descendants of the Native Americans worked by British settlers before the arrival of large numbers of Africans—remained enslaved. If Johnson were part black, as Laurens suggested in his letter to Grant, the overseer may well have been a product of a South Carolina family or community where close relationships formed across color lines and among the free and enslaved.

Johnson and/or his parents might have been enslaved, working either as field hands or as drivers, men who kept their fellow slaves on task. In such a scenario, Johnson would have gained extensive plantation experience. If Johnson was from a family of Settlement Indians, he could also have obtained farming skills as a hired laborer or as a farmer in his community. Alternatively, Johnson might have hailed from a backcountry region in which farming helped sustain a trading post. Such locales—notably George Galphin's Silver Bluff—supported mixed populations. Galphin, an Indian trader with a native wife by whom he had several children, planted indigo and other crops at Silver Bluff, using slaves that in time would include his children by a black bondswoman.[29] However Johnson acquired his farming and management skills, he put them to excellent use during his brief tenure at Mount Oswald: Grant and other East Florida planters who served as

Oswald's eyes and ears were extremely impressed with Johnson's labors.[30] His flight from Mount Oswald was a mystery and a nuisance to Laurens and a challenge for Oswald, who needed to replace Johnson with an equally able overseer. Although he did not remain at the plantation long enough to see indigo flourish there, Johnson's efforts, in concert with those of the slaves he managed, created the conditions for success. Indeed, not long after Johnson's departure, Oswald learned that his land had been rendered productive and brought in more slaves and several "white overseers to enhance security and direct daily activities."[31]

Why Did Johnson Leave?

The historical record offers no direct clues as to why Johnson left, although several indirect clues point to East Florida as a potential harbor for an Indian or person of Indian and African heritage. When East Florida was a Spanish possession, Spaniards sought to undermine their British neighbors' stability by offering South Carolina slaves freedom at St. Augustine. Although Spanish imperialism was as fraught with human injustice as British practices were, the Spaniards created more malleable social relations between colonizer and colonized: if Indians and blacks embraced Christianity, they secured the possibility of living more on their own terms. Indeed, both in St. Augustine and at nearby Fort Mose, a free black town established in 1738, former slaves and the Indians with whom they intermarried lived as their own masters. Although a number of black and Indian communities were evacuated to Cuba when the Spanish left East Florida in 1763, others stayed, and escaped slaves from South Carolina and Georgia continued to find refuge with East Florida Indians.[32] Thus especially around St. Augustine, less than fifty miles from Mount Oswald, Johnson might have found a home where he was beholden to no one but himself.

Johnson might also have chosen to live in an Indian settlement less bound up within black and white cultures. Mount Oswald was built on the grounds of what had been a large Timucuan Indian settlement, Nocoroco,[33] and although the number of Timucuas and other peoples native to East Florida had dropped precipitously, Yuchis (likely descendants of East Florida aborigines), Yamassees from South Carolina, and Creeks from Georgia (called Seminoles in East Florida) had settlements throughout the colony. Indeed, during Grant's tenure as governor of East Florida, naturalists John and William Bartram had vivid encounters with Indians, and William's published travelogue includes descriptions of East Florida Indian villages with lush agricultural lands rich with foodstuffs.[34] Perhaps Johnson used his farming skills at one such site.

Mount Oswald and other indigo plantations in East Florida, Georgia, and South Carolina formed a major component of the British imperial project in the Southeast: many thousands of acres of Indian land were taken and ultimately given over to the crop, and many thousands of African as well as a smaller number of Indian slaves were forced to tend indigo and produce dye. In a brief but notable moment in the history of this imperialism, an Indian man with possible African blood decided to walk away from this blue matrix of conquest and domination. Although the historical record does not show what became of him, colonial East Florida offered him opportunities to choose a path that may have empowered him greatly.

CHAPTER 7 ❧ Slave John Williams

A Key Contributor to the Lucas-Pinckney Indigo Concern

DURING MOST OF THE 1750s, after she had produced excellent indigo on her father's South Carolina plantations, planter and amateur botanist Eliza Lucas Pinckney lived in England with her family, and at some point just prior to that sojourn, she created a beautiful wrap for herself (illus. 9).[1] With painstaking, careful stitches, she crafted a looping, curving pattern of vines with delicate leaves, producing a veritable garden of foliage in which she might immerse herself. She chose to depict indigo plants on her wrap, and it is easy to imagine that this gorgeous textile was her personal tribute to her success with the staple, which enriched her family; her home, South Carolina; and Britain, her nation. She undoubtedly wore her wrap in the company of others and may have delighted in telling companions about her experiments in cultivating the plant: then as now, many people saw Eliza Lucas Pinckney as bound up in indigo. During her lifetime, she was recognized for her work with the crop; while in England, she showcased her pride in it by presenting the dowager Princess of Wales with indigo-colored birds; and upon her return to South Carolina, she lived where it grew, even as her estates and fortune diminished during and after the Revolutionary War.[2]

Pinckney's wrap is not blue but white, the typical hue for such a garment of the period. However, just like the color white, the wrap in a sense contains many colors. The blue dye plants featured in the textile were produced via the work of several white people as well as the work of black and red slaves. The toil of extracting the dye from indigo and the people who did this backbreaking work are present but invisible in Pinckney's finely wrought wrap.

However, Lucas and Pinckney family documents as well as colonial records bring to light the names of some of the slaves who performed this crucial labor.

Clues in these documents have enabled me to draw a portrait of one such slave, Quash, who proved instrumental in helping the Lucas-Pinckney clan achieve success with indigo. Eliza Lucas Pinckney depended on Quash, a mulatto slave carpenter who was likely the driver on Wappoo, the plantation where she first grew indigo. This man, ultimately christened John Williams, was her trusted associate as well as the artisan who made the wooden vats that ensured the production of fine-quality dye. Moreover, Williams helped provide Charles and Eliza Pinckney with a Charles Town home that reflected their stature as important planters and influential members of South Carolina society.

Additional period documents provide less complete but still noteworthy information about other slaves who contributed to the Lucas-Pinckney indigo concern. Because these laborers were field hands and house slaves whose efforts to run the plantation and home were largely taken for granted, their names are recorded only when they are connected with specific financial transactions or counted in inventories as possessions. Although their lives are thus sketched merely in outline, they nevertheless can be firmly recovered.[3]

A Young White Woman Takes on Indigo

Eliza Lucas Pinckney is a key figure in the history of South Carolina indigo not only because she was among the very first to cultivate the dye plant but also because as a female planter, she was atypical and therefore noteworthy. Although other colonial women worked outside the home—Nicola Phillips documents women's prevalence in eighteenth-century business, Beverly Lemire reveals their significant place in the huge garment industry, and Mary Ferrari describes their presence in Charles Town enterprises[4]—the popular image of an eighteenth-century female from the planter class is that of a largely decorative grand dame who produced children for aristocratic dynasties. Eliza Lucas Pinckney is in fact remembered for birthing sons who were key participants in South Carolina and early U.S. history,[5] but she also shines as a major agricultural innovator.

Pinckney had success with her indigo experiments not only because of her intrepidness but also because the property where she first cultivated the plant was established on rich land and because several free and many enslaved people contributed resources and expertise to her venture. Her first indigo-growing plantation was Wappoo, named for the creek on which it depended for irriga-tion, transportation, and water for dye making. The creek, in turn, was named for an indigenous people who no longer roamed the area after their numbers shrank as a consequence of colonist-introduced disease.[6] Eliza Lucas Pinckney's grandfather, John Lucas, had acquired Wappoo in 1714.[7] At that time, most resi-dents of the Charles Town area were black slaves brought in to work plantations, although natives and whites were also present.[8]

By 1738, Wappoo had passed into the hands of John Lucas's son, George, who brought most of his family, including his daughter, Eliza, with him from Antigua to live at Wappoo. Within a year George Lucas had purchased two additional plantations, one on the Combahee River near what is now Beaufort and one on the Waccamaw River near today's Georgetown. He placed these properties in the hands of hired white overseers and then mortgaged the plantations, following his practice at Wappoo and in Antigua, and used the funds to advance his military career.[9] Shortly thereafter, George Lucas returned to Antigua to serve in the war commencing with Spain, and his military post, followed by his appointment as the island's lieutenant governor, kept him from returning to South Carolina. When he left the colony, he charged his seventeen-year-old daughter, Eliza, with the care not only of his South Carolina holdings but also of her mother and sis-ter. Eliza Lucas found herself in the common but frowned upon position of run-ning a plantation with too few white males (none in her case) in the household.[10] Eliza Lucas had several white neighbors, including Andrew Deveaux, whom she contacted regularly about indigo and other matters,[11] but she spent most of her time with her mother, who frequently took to her bed; her young sister, whom Eliza strove to see educated; and more than twenty slaves.

Sales records from Wappoo combine with family correspondence to paint a general picture of the plantation at this time,[12] and the letters suggest why Lucas has become so noteworthy: she was an extremely resourceful and committed planter. Wappoo consisted of the home that the young girl occupied with her family, a barn, outbuildings, six hundred acres of land, and stands of trees planted by her slaves at her direction. Although she lacked the training and networks of an established botanist such as Alexander Garden, who became her friend and admirer,[13] Lucas acquired a great deal of knowledge about plants through her own initiative, and when given responsibility for her father's plantations, she worked eagerly to cultivate and beautify them. A botany enthusiast, she wrote letters full of observations about and delight in native vegetation as well as details regarding her efforts to get Caribbean plants to thrive in South Carolina.[14]

Lucas's letterbook also suggests that profit drove the young woman to make her father's three South Carolina plantations productive. Lucas was not only a dutiful daughter complying with her father's wishes but a person determined to bring fortune and honor to all that signaled home to her: her immediate family, the family into which she married, the colony of South Carolina, and her nation. Lucas's motivation resulted not from an abstract ideological imperative, however, but from financial instability: her father had incurred substantial debt.[15] Mortgaging his property to purchase a coveted military commission may have furthered George Lucas's standing and political ambition, but doing so also put pressure on his agricultural estates to turn a profit. He gambled that his South Carolina plantations would produce income since the profits from his sugar plantations, like others in Antigua, were decreasing.[16] George Lucas spent only a brief time in the southern colony investigating its potential but seemed sure enough of it as an investment—and of his daughter as his surrogate—to send seed to her from several crop plants that grew in Antigua with which she might experiment.

A Black Helpmate alongside White Associates

As Eliza Lucas thought about which Caribbean staples might flourish in the South Carolina low country, she drew not only on expertise she acquired as a self-taught student of all things botanical but also on the knowledge and work of other people. Lucas wrote that she spent some time in her fields every day, but she certainly was not supervising all of the work performed there: that job would have been handled by a driver.[17] Although her letters do not name her driver, it was most likely Quash, a mulatto slave carpenter. According to Joyce E. Chaplin, eighteenth-century travelers in the Lower South observed that black drivers frequently "managed much of the day-to-day direction of agricultural activities."[18] In his work on eighteenth-century slave life, Philip D. Morgan points out that "one identifiable type" of driver was a slave tradesman, a person who would far exceed the appraised value of other slaves because he played two critical roles on a plantation.[19] An entry in Eliza Lucas's 1742 letterbook suggests that she had close ties to Quash: when he was accused of having tried to run off, she "was at his trial when he proved himself quite Innocent."[20] South Carolina had experienced a major slave revolt, the Stono Rebellion, three years earlier, and slaves found guilty of crimes in the colony were treated harshly: Eliza Lucas noted that the ringleader of the episode in which Quash was accused "is to be hanged and one [participant] Whyped."[21] Moreover, among the eighty-eight slaves in Antigua executed in 1737 for conspiring against their masters was George Lucas's Cesar, who perished by fire.[22] Eliza Lucas's advocacy on behalf of Quash, implicitly by attending his trial and explicitly in her letter to her father, suggests that he was tied to the family by much more than his value as chattel. He appears to have been a trusted and valued member of her household and business concerns, a slave with whom she worked closely.

Quash certainly had an active role in the success of Eliza Lucas's indigo project, which she undertook with the assistance of other slaves and some free people. These experiments with the dye plant are described in Lucas's early 1740s letterbook entries and in a 1785 missive to her son, Charles Cotesworth Pinckney.[23] Further details can be gleaned from other records. Eliza Lucas first had indigo seed planted in the summer of 1740; the resulting crop was largely taken by frost, but her slaves harvested some seed, which they grew the following summer. Although her 1741 yield was low, she had enough plants to discuss with her neighbor, Andrew Deveaux, who was also experimenting with indigo, and with which dye maker Nicholas Cromwell could work. Cromwell was a white contract laborer who hired himself out; George Lucas had sent Cromwell from Montserrat to teach Eliza and two family slaves how to make dye cakes from indigo plants.[24]

Montserrat, an English possession in the Caribbean, was known for producing indigo. The island was populated by English and Irish settlers as well as numerous black slaves. In 1737, just before the Lucases went to South Carolina, these slaves were subjected to strict laws that curtailed what had been a degree of freedom to grow and sell agricultural products, including indigo.[25] The measure clearly represented an attempt by white Montserrat inhabitants to curtail the access to the money and marginal autonomy these enslaved persons had accrued. George Lucas's search for a dye maker confirms that the island's black population had developed a reputation for real skill with indigo: before committing to Cromwell, Lucas tried to get a "Negro" indigo dye maker from the island.[26]

Although Cromwell fulfilled his contractual obligations to the Lucas family, he also appears to have sabotaged his own efforts and the Lucases' ambitions, which were ultimately realized not only through Eliza Lucas's continued efforts but also through those of her new husband, Charles Pinckney, and especially through Quash's labors. Eliza Lucas reported that Cromwell "made some brick Vats on my Fathers plantation on Wappoo Creek" but that he also made "a great mistery" of the dye-making process by adding too much lime.[27] Despite this setback—perhaps the result of the dye maker's remorse over sharing indigo techniques that kept Montserrat in dye production[28]—the young woman had her slaves undertake subsequent plantings. In both 1742 and 1743, Wappoo produced little indigo, but the following year, with the aid of Nicholas Cromwell's more reliable brother, Patrick, Lucas's slaves made a good quantity of dye. She then had her overseer at the Lucas Garden Hill Plantation on the Combahee cultivating indigo, another project that met with great success.[29]

When Eliza Lucas married Charles Pinckney in 1744, he accepted a modest dowry—the mortgaged Wappoo and its slaves—which indicates George Lucas's limited means.[30] Later in the year, Eliza Pinckney told her father that her husband had begun the necessary steps to get the family's indigo onto the English market by sending six pounds of her dye to London to be evaluated.[31] It was received there with favor: a December 3 letter to Charles Pinckney published in the April 1, 1745, issue of the *South Carolina Gazette* states that "one of our most noted brokers [had] tried it against some of the best French, and his opinion it is as good. . . . When you can in some measure supply the British demand, we are persuaded, that on proper application to Parliament, a duty will be laid on foreign growth, for I am informed, that we pay for indigo to the French £200,000 per annum."[32]

Although George Lucas was no doubt pleased with his daughter's accomplishments, he remained concerned about the quality of dye produced on his plantations. He continued to employ Nicholas Cromwell's services despite his disreputable nature and questions about the reliability of his brick vats but looked for alternatives, including a "Negro dye maker" from Montserrat.[33] This effort shows not only that the planter knew that such workers were very skilled but also that he expected a slave to be more compliant than Cromwell. Lucas ultimately gave up on Nicholas Cromwell and turned to Quash at the end of 1744, writing to Charles Pinckney on December 24,

I have since recollected upon my wife telling me the indigo Nicholas Cromwell made gave linen a red cast, that it may be possibly continue some time, if not always, as the work is made of bricks. I therefore desire Quashy may be put immediately, to make an indigo work of the same dimensions, with the brick one at Wappoo on Garden Hill Plantation, with plank and timber, the plank to be well joined, and pin'd [?], with wood to the frame of the inside, that it may be tried there with a small quantity of ground, planted there, and if a difference appears, another such work may be made at Wappoo.[34]

Although Patrick Cromwell had produced good dye from brick vats, Lucas did not trust them and charged Quash with improving the family's indigo concern.

Garden Hill's first successful crop may well have been indigo produced in 1745 after Quash completed the wooden dye works there. Garden Hill overseer William Murray's account sheet for that year shows that he shipped to Lucas's London agent indigo valued at more than £225.[35] Charles Pinckney's accounts show that by 1746, the Lucas-Pinckney clan preferred wood to brick in their indigo operations, and at one point in the later 1740s, Quash spent thirty-three days making wooden indigo vats at Garden Hill and elsewhere.[36] Pinckney's records thus establish that Quash's carpentry skills made a key contribution to the Lucas-Pinckney indigo experiments.

Other documents written by Charles Pinckney in the mid- to late 1740s also show the extraordinary skills that Quash possessed. Pinckney and George Lucas quietly battled for the use of Quash's services. Sometime between late 1744 and the spring of 1745, Lucas instructed Pinckney to insure Quash and send him by a "prime sailer" to Antigua.[37] Pinckney demurred, arguing that he had great use for the slave, and on May 22, 1745, Lucas relented, nevertheless maintaining that he could "make considerably more of [Quash's] labor."[38] Later that year, Pinckney began purchasing materials for a city residence in Charles Town, and in 1746, he put Quash in charge of the entire construction project. On a November 4, 1746, list of building specifications that Pinckney wrote out for Quash, the planter concluded, "In your calculation you are desired to distinguish and set down what the Carpenters work comes to; what the Joiners, including the Dining room and what without the dining room, and what the stairs & Venetian window separately come to."[39] These instructions not only describe a stately home with a great deal of woodwork but also demonstrate that the slave read, wrote, and kept accounts. Quash also was paid well for overseeing the ambitious building project:

Pinckney's account book indicates that Quash received "3 years & 3 months allowance at £200 pr. annum from 1st Jan. 1746 to 1st April 1750,—£650."[40]

Pinckney also paid Quash on three separate occasions "to encourage him in his carving work."[41] Such payments suggest that in addition to managing the large construction project, Quash applied his woodworking skills in the building of the Pinckney home. Although the house burned down in Charles Town's great fire of 1861, a family member later published a lengthy description of its features, including its woodwork:

> The window on [the] staircase (one of the most remarkable features of the house) was very beautiful, of three arches with heavily carved frames, and a deep window-seat extending the whole length of the landing-place. . . . The whole house was wainscoted in the heaviest paneling, the windows and doors with deep projecting pediments and mouldings in the style of Chamberlayne. The mantelpieces were very high and narrow, with fronts carved in processions of shepherds and shepherdesses, cupids, etc., and had square frames in the paneling above, to be filled with pictures.[42]

One additional notation in Pinckney's list of building expenditures demonstrates how highly the planter valued his carpenter. After George Lucas's death, his South Carolina properties were foreclosed, and Pinckney purchased Quash and a few other Wappoo slaves. The deed that records the sale also identifies Quash as John Williams, and on May 12, 1750, Pinckney manumitted Williams.[43] More than any other financial transaction, this document demonstrates Charles and Eliza Pinckney's esteem for John Williams. Eliza witnessed and signed the manumission document that Charles composed: "Now know ye that the said Charles Pinckney in consideration of the good faithfull service of the said John Williams heretofore done and performed and for diverse other good causes [?] and valueable considerations one thereunto especially moving . . . do mannumise and set free the said John Williams by whatsoever name he may heretofore have been known or called from all slavery bondage and restraint to me whatsoever."[44] Whatever services Williams rendered that persuaded Charles and Eliza Pinckney to free their slave, his professional skills as an overseer and carpenter were obviously crucial to the Lucas and Pinckney families' accomplishments. Moreover, at a time when very few people of color were free or financially well-off in South Carolina, Williams was both. A July 1750 deed shows that the Reverend Alexander Garden, leader of the Anglican Church in Charles Town and the man who baptized Williams in 1746, purchased two subdivisions of four town lots from the Pinckneys on behalf of the former slave.[45] Williams had Garden hold these lots in trust for his daughters Amy, Mary, and Sabina, two of whom he bought out of slavery for two hundred pounds in 1751.[46] In less than ten years, Williams acquired additional land, arranging for partial repayment of Garden's loan with four hundred acres near the mouth of Santee River.[47] This 1758 transaction listed Williams as a carpenter and planter (and therefore a slave owner) in St. James Parish, and a 1763 record shows that he owned six hundred acres along the Santee, although the notice also indicates that he needed to sell that property and leave South Carolina.[48]

Other Black and Red Contributors

If John Williams's final circumstances remain mysterious, the entire lives of the other slaves who worked the Lucas and Pinckney plantations at first appear even more so. Snippets of information appear when the slaves are listed as property in financial records or when the enslaved persons' skills were desired or marketable. For example, each slave is recorded by name in appendixes to plantation deeds, and some such lists include information about whether a person was a field hand or an artisan.[49] Further, the letters in which George Lucas and Charles Pinckney politely vie for Quash's carpentry skills also refer to a cook named Dick whose services both white men sought. Moreover, Pinckney kept careful records when he hired out slaves, especially for his house slave, Bettina, and "Nurse Molly," who did considerable work for others while he and his family lived in England. These brief notices not only mark people as chattel but at times give a sense of their skill and effort: Dick delighted palates, Bettina kept a very clean house, Molly healed the sick. Other records illustrate that along with Quash, Barbuda, C. Quaca, N. Quaca, Pompey, Quamina, Say, and Sogo were woodworkers; Pompey was Quash's apprentice.[50]

Additional family records provide racial designations for a few of these enslaved people. "Indian Peter" must have been entirely or part Native American, as were Mary Ann and her two children, Prince and Beck, since Mary Ann was labeled a *mustee*.[51] Both Dick and Quash were described as mulattos.[52] The origins of these mixed-race slaves, like the backgrounds of Wappoo's other bondspeople, are undocumented. However, given that the Wappoo slaves were originally owned by John Lucas, an absentee landowner, they were likely acquired in South Carolina and very possibly born there. And although some Caribbean-born mulattos were sold at the Charles Town slave market, the Lucas-Pinckney mulattos were more likely the product of a South Carolina white planter's or overseer's sexual relations with a slave woman.[53] Quash and Wappoo's other mulatto slaves could even have been the offspring of the man who oversaw the plantation on behalf of John Lucas: if they were born shortly after Lucas acquired the property in 1714, they would have been in their early twenties when Eliza Lucas took over the plantation in 1739.

Although Lucas-Pinckney family records explicitly offer only scant data about slaves other than Quash/John Williams, they do show that twenty slaves were needed to run the successful indigo operation and plantation home at Wappoo: Williams, Dick, Mary Ann, Dick, Lynn, Sawney, Indian Peter, Isaac, Pompey, Sarah, Mo, Beck, Molly, Nanny, Mary, Peter, Pompey, Douglas, Betty, and little Gulla.[54] Some of these slaves helped produce indigo, while others worked as house slaves, thereby indirectly aiding the planters' indigo concerns.

The skills, knowledge, and labor of black and Indian slaves were thus crucial to the Lucas-Pinckney family's successful dye-making endeavor and to family members' lives more broadly. And although the white planters clearly saw their slaves as chattel, generally referring to them only as property rather than as human beings, these references can provide much more information about slave life at Wappoo than at first seems apparent. Moreover, Charles and Eliza Pinckney's treatment of John Williams indicates that they knew the value that he in particular—and undoubtedly other slaves as well—added to their lives. They would not have been able to make blue without red and black.

CONCLUSION ❧ South Carolina Indigo
A History of Color

IN ADDITION TO COLORING CLOTH, eighteenth-century indigo was used to make ink and in bluing (the process of whitening paper or fabric). Making ink was a rather straightforward process: ground indigo was added to lampblack (the chief ingredient for eighteenth-century ink) to produce an ink with rich, dark color. However, the overriding effect was black rather than blue, and over time, the color fades to brown, meaning that extant documents written with such ink now bear no visible link to the dye plant.[1] Paper was made from rags during the eighteenth century, and a dingy, yellowish cast to both paper and cloth could be corrected with an indigo wash, creating a bright white appearance.[2] Despite its name, bluing is a kind of bleaching.

These two uses indicate that indigo can be found in paper and ink records of the period as well as in eighteenth-century clothing that does not itself seem blue, an idea that I find marvelous. But its invisibility in these instances is also somewhat disquieting. There is no easy way to see and experience the dye in many artifacts from the time that concerns this book. Such ghostly traces do not clearly index the widespread use of the dye.

I started this book with my fascination at the lush blue in a beautiful dress at the Museum of London, a garment displayed with hidden supports that made it seem both full and empty. The book also concluded with a garment—Eliza Lucas Pinckney's white wrap decorated with indigo plants—and the unseen. I think of the beautiful white textile as a tabula rasa on which another fabric can be viewed: the social fabric comprised of the red, white, and black peoples who made indigo culture in colonial South Carolina.

Both the dress and the wrap remained ever present in my mind as I began learning about indigo and its uses; so too, was a sense of wanting to see—to see the indigo I was reading about, to see the indigo that had faded from period texts I studied, and especially to see invisible histories in indigo's rise to prominence in eighteenth-century South Carolina. To assuage that feeling, I began a project with ethnobotanist Karen Hall and costume historian and designer Kendra Johnson, both of whom have great expertise with plants, dyes, and clothing and share my interest in varied South Carolina histories. We sought to grow indigo, make dye from it, and color a garment with that dye. At the same time, Karen was also in the midst of a long-term project in which she, Cherokee colleagues, and landscape architects were collaborating to create a Cherokee Worldview Garden at the South Carolina Botanical Garden, and Kendra was involved in creating reproduction eighteenth- and nineteenth-century slave garments to exhibit locally. The two projects shared the goal of creating highly visible and very beautiful tributes to the lifeways of Native Americans and enslaved Africans and African Americans, creating living histories for these peoples in South Carolina.

One of our joint endeavors was to dye a portion of Kendra's reproduction eighteenth-century slave skirt with indigo (illus. 10). Kendra had made the skirt with the heavy and coarse wool that slaves of the period would have worn in colder months, and when we submerged the garment in the dye, it drank the liquid like a sponge. Repeated dunking saw the material absorb even more of the color until it reached a warm, deep blue. The skirt took a long time to dry and colored a bit unevenly because of its thick folds and the relatively small size of our vat. Nevertheless, I found it as beautiful as Eliza Lucas Pinckney's wrap and the London silk dress.

I thought the skirt lovely not only because I admire Kendra, who made it, as well as Karen, who prepared the indigo vat that dyed it, but also because helping to color the item gave me a small but significant way to see the blue I had researched, thought about, and written about. When we swirled the skirt in the rich, greenish liquid, it seemed incredible that the wool would ultimately become blue. When we pulled the skirt from the vat and the garment came into contact with oxygen, the glorious transformation I had read about in books unfolded spectacularly. I found it magical that something invisible could have such a profound effect and was in fact necessary to make blue. Through this wonderful process, the ghostly absences that I had felt, worked to unearth, and was putting onto paper became present. I saw them.

The past is not a singular phenomenon to be recovered but a social fabric to be woven from diverse historical strands to become a means to clothe the present with knowledge and foresight. Today's South Carolina was shaped by numerous factors, including the making of blue in the colonial period. Indigo's incursion into South Carolina was multifaceted, and the culture that arose from the plant and its dye was complex. Indigo helped some South Carolinians become wealthy and see themselves as learned, patrician gentlemen yet subjected others to burdensome labor in noisome circumstances. Indigo ignited the curiosity and interest of those who loved and studied plants, allowing them to accrue intellectual as well as monetary capital, yet contributed to the alienation of natives from their land. The shrub enriched many lives but simultaneously impoverished many others.

South Carolina's Janus-faced indigo culture becomes less dichotomous and more complex with respect to clothing because indigo-dyed garments simultaneously represent and embody multiple conditions of colonial experience. Broadly, such clothing indexes staple production, manufacturing processes, and trade loops: blue items worn in South Carolina between the mid-1750s and the Revolutionary War were often made in Britain from cloth colored there by dye from the colony and then shipped back across the Atlantic. Blue garments could enable individuals to at least appear to be of greater social standing than they otherwise would have merited: for example, a hand-me-down blue frock worn by a house slave at home defined its wearer as higher-status bondswoman; off of her master's property, the garment could enable her to pass as a free person. Further, a blue matchcoat defined its wearer as an Indian, but when worn proudly along with additional handsome fittings, it helped make that Indian stand out as a person to be reckoned with.

Indigo blue also appears on the South Carolina state flag, another textile with great relevance for a meditation on color in the state today. The deep blue flag with a white crescent and palmetto tree honors Colonel William Moultrie and the members of his Second South Carolina Regiment, who wore crescents on their caps and blue uniforms as they defended Charles Town against the British during the Revolutionary War by building a fort from palmetto logs.[3] In 2008, the flag's blue background and the fact that that it recalls Moultrie's men's uniforms helped to inspire a South Carolina girl to propose that the state make indigo blue its official color. She also chose indigo because the plant had been a major cash crop in the colonial period. Picking up on this thread, a state senator remarked that Eliza Lucas Pinckney had been one of the primary developers of indigo as a South Carolina staple, and he lauded the girl who suggested the idea as another young woman committed to making indigo a part of South Carolina's history.[4]

So the state color is now indigo, and Moultrie and Eliza Pinckney—who in 1989 became the first woman inducted into the state business hall of fame—are the historical persons referenced in short blurbs about the state color. Few popular sources discuss Moultrie's participation in Colonel James Grant's campaign against the Cherokees, during which their towns and agricultural fields were destroyed, or mention that Moultrie and the Second South Carolina Regiment killed or captured numerous runaway slaves.[5] Further, publications that discuss Eliza Pinckney's work with indigo fail to discuss the individual African and Indian slaves who were integral to her efforts.

Those of us who live in South Carolina owe it to ourselves, to those who came before us, and to those who come after to plumb the depths and examine the expanse of events that color our past and that shape our present. The more we understand about South Carolina Indian and African culture and the ways in which they intertwined with one another and with the culture of the state's European colonizers, the more we can see that the past here was complicated, both terrible and empowering. Fully understanding these complications will help us ensure that we repeat only the best of what came before and that we never again enact injustices like those that burdened and broke so many. Red, black, and white made the blue of South Carolina's state flag. I hope that all of this state's colors, past and present, find their histories, learn from them, and move forward to make room for richness and complexity. These qualities can be found in South Carolina indigo, and our flag can represent both.

NOTES

INTRODUCTION *Why South Carolina Indigo?*

1. Michel Pastoureau, *Blue: The History of a Color* (Princeton: Princeton University Press, 2001), 123.

2. "Blue—Blues," *Dictionary of Traded Goods and Commodities, 1550–1820* (2007), accessed March 25, 2011, http://www.british-history.ac.uk/report.aspx?compid=58704.

3. For a nuanced discussion of how environment shaped cultivation in regions that abut South Carolina, see Mart A. Stewart, *"What Nature Suffers to Groe": Life, Labor, and Landscape on the Georgia Coast, 1680–1920* (Athens: University of Georgia Press, 1996).

4. Following Rachel N. Klein and eighteenth-century South Carolinians, I employ the term *backcountry* to designate "the entire area beyond the nineteen coastal parishes, the most recent of which (Prince Frederick) had been created in 1734. [An] entire area [that] included only one vaguely defined parish, which sent one representative to the colonial assembly" (*Unification of a Slave State: The Rise of the Planter Class in the South Carolina Backcountry, 1760–1808* [Chapel Hill: University of North Carolina Press for the Institute of Early American History and Culture, 1990], 7). Following Daniel K. Richter, I use the term *Indian Country* to describe the "vast majority of eastern North America [that] was neither English nor French nor Spanish territory" (*Facing East from Indian Country: A Native History of Early America* [Cambridge: Harvard University Press, 2001], 2).

5. Hannah Arendt, *The Human Condition* (Chicago: University of Chicago Press, 1958), 136.

6. Anthropologist Igor Kopytoff's "processual" approach to the study of things helps me frame my study in particularly active terms; he maintains that writing an object's "biography" is the best way to account for its multiple transformations, meanings, and effects in varied situations ("The Cultural Biography of Things: Commoditization as Process," in *The Social Life of Things: Commodities in Cultural Perspective*, ed. Arjun Appadurai [Cambridge:

University Press, 1986], 64–91). I also embrace sociologist Ian Woodward's ̷ment to understanding things as entities that produce symbolic meanings within ̷ir structure but that equally create social meanings based on how people enlist them in social performances (*Understanding Material Culture* [Los Angeles: Sage, 2007], 173). I interpret these interactions in light of archeologist Andrew Jones's belief, following philosopher-anthropologist Bruno Latour's argument, that material goods' and persons' relationships are not cyclical, with people acting on things and then things acting on people; rather, object-human relations are "interstitial"—that is, "held together in and through action" (Andrew Jones, *Memory and Material Culture* [Cambridge: Cambridge University Press, 2007], 37).

7. Laurel Thatcher Ulrich, *The Age of Homespun: Objects and Stories in the Creation of an American Myth* (New York: Vintage, 2001).

8. Joan Scott, "After History?," paper presented at the History and Limits of Interpretation Conference, Rice University, Houston, March 15–17, 1996.

9. Ibid.; Michael Foucault, "Nietzsche, Genealogy, History," in *Language, Counter-Memory, Practice: Selected Essays and Interviews*, ed. Donald F. Bouchard (Ithaca: Cornell University Press, 1977), 154.

10. Scott, "After History."

11. Ibid.

12. Karl Kroeber, "Unaesthetic Imaginings: Native American Myth as Speech Genre," *boundary 2* 23, no. 2 (1996): 171–97.

13. Ibid., 181.

CHAPTER 1. *South Carolina Indigo in British Textiles for the Home and Colonial Market*

1. Ambrose Heal, *The Signboards of Old London Shops* (New York: Blom, 1972), 62.

2. Heal's book reproduces several "Indian queen" signs and several "black boy" signs. The former hung at a variety of different establishments: at a dyer's, a linen draper's, four mercer's shops, and a playing card maker's establishment. "Black boy" signs were placed out front of a haberdasher's shop, a laceman's, a linen draper's, and in combination with a still at a tobacconist's. "Black boys" with feathers at their heads and/or waists are sometimes identified as "blackamoors" in signs for linen drapers and other establishments, some related to clothing. See Heal, *Signboards*, 51–169.

3. For an overview of the varied plants that produce blue dyes, see Jenny Balfour-Paul, *Indigo* (London: Archetype, 2006), 89–96.

4. Ibid., 27–28. Woad, which grew in Northern Europe, including Britain, was the chief blue dye for clothing until the fifteenth century, when the sea route opened to India made indigo from the East less expensive (Dauril Alden, "The Growth and Decline of Indigo Production in Colonial Brazil: A Study in Comparative Economic History," *Journal of Economic History* 25, no. 1 [1965]: 37).

5. Michel Pastoureau, *Blue: The History of a Color* (Princeton: Princeton University Press, 2001), 123.

6. Ibid., 134.

7. See John J. Winberry, "Reputation of Carolina Indigo," *South Carolina Historical Magazine* 80, no. 3 (1979): 242–50; S. Max Edelson, "The Characters of Commodities: The Reputation of South Carolina Rice and Indigo in the Atlantic World," in *The Atlantic Economy during the Seventeenth and Eighteenth Centuries: Organization, Operation, Practice, and Personnel*, ed. Peter A. Coclanis (Columbia: University of South Carolina Press, 2005), 349–55.

8. Many pamphleteers were self-styled opinion makers who sought to influence public debate through their publications.

9. [John Ledyard], *Methods for Improving the Manufacture of Indigo: Originally Submitted to the Consideration of the Carolina Planters; and Now Published for the Benefit of All the British Colonies, Whose Situation Is Favorable to the Culture of Indigo. To Which Are Added, Several Public and Private Letters, Relating to the Same Subject* (Devizes, 1776).

10. Ibid., 9.

11. Barnett A. Elzas, *The Jews of South Carolina: From the Earliest Times to the Present Day* (Philadelphia: Lippincott, 1905), 47–67; Charles Reznikoff with Uriah Z. Engelman, *The Jews of Charleston: A History of an American Jewish Community* (Philadelphia: Jewish Publication Society of America, 1950), 23–34.

12. Lindo letter excerpted in Ledyard, *Methods for Improving the Manufacture of Indigo*, 33.

13. Anonymous planter letter excerpted in ibid., 21

14. Laurens showed his dye to London brokers and dyers without revealing its origins; they took it to be East Florida indigo, a type typically well regarded (Henry Laurens to Gabriel Manigault, March 20, 1772, in *The Papers of Henry Laurens*, vol. 8, October 10, 1771–April 19, 1773, ed. David R. Chesnutt [Columbia: University of South Carolina Press, 1980], 228).

15. Max S. Edelson, *Plantation Enterprise in Colonial South Carolina* (Cambridge: Harvard University Press, 2006), 185; Edelson, "Characters of Commodities," 353. Laurens had mixed feelings about Lindo's work as South Carolina's dye inspector:

although Laurens endorsed Lindo's enterprise and used his services, the inspector did not grade some of Laurens's product as favorably as he must have wished (Henry Laurens to Cowles and Harford, October 12, 1762, in *The Papers of Henry Laurens*, vol. 3, January 1, 1759–August 31, 1763, ed. David R. Chesnutt [Columbia: University of South Carolina Press, 1972] 131n8).

16. *Morning Chronicle and London Advertiser*, July 25, 1775.

17. Alden, "Growth and Decline"; R. Haller, "The Production of Indigo," *Ciba Review* 85 (April 1951): 3074; David McCreery, "Indigo Commodity Chains in the Spanish and British Empires, 1560–1860," in *From Silver to Cocaine: Latin American Commodity Chains and the Building of the World Economy*, ed. Steven Topik, Carlos Marichal, and Zephyr Frank (Durham: Duke University Press, 2006), 66–67.

18. Edelson, "Characters of Commodities," 352.

19. Virginia Jelatis, "Tangled Up in Blue: Indigo Culture and Economy in South Carolina, 1747–1800" (PhD diss., University of Minnesota, 1999), 200–201, uses several period sources to carefully calculate the amounts and values of indigo exported from South Carolina to Britain from 1747 to 1775. The later 1750s, 1768, and 1770–75 were particularly lucrative years.

20. A review of British newspapers advertising indigo sales in London from 1748 until the Revolutionary War shows that the bulk of the indigo on offer came from Carolina (*General Advertiser*, February 6, August 16, 19, September 22, 28, 1748, February 19, 1749; *London Gazetteer*, March 15, 1749; *Public Advertiser*, October 21, 1755, January 10, 1756, March 2, October 13, 26, 31, 1757; *Morning Chronicle and London Advertiser*, April 19, 1774, November 17, December 15, 1775; *Public Ledger*, June 22, 1775; *Morning Chronicle and London Advertiser*, January 10, March 2, 29, 1775).

21. Winberry, "Reputation of Carolina Indigo," 244. For a discussion of preparing cloth for domestic and foreign markets and issues of quality in finishing, see John Smail, *Merchants, Markets, and Manufacture: The English Wool Textile Industry in the Eighteenth Century* (Basingstoke: Palgrave Macmillan, 1999), 61–68, 138–41. For general information on eighteenth-century dyeing, see John Edmonds, *The History and Practice of Eighteenth Century Dyeing* (Little Chalfont: Edmonds, 1999); D. B. Dagley, *Mark Thornhill Wade, Silk Dyer, Soho* (London: Research Publishing, 1961).

22. For a discussion of common wear and its relationships to elite costume and Indian textiles, see Beverly Lemire, *Fashion's Favourite: The Cotton Trade and the Consumer in Britain, 1660–1800* (Oxford: Oxford University Press for the Pasold Research Fund, 1991).

23. Lemire, *Fashion's Favourite*, details the growth of fashionable lightweight fabrics in Britain. See also Beverly Lemire, "Fashioning Cottons: Asian Trade, Domestic Industry, and Consumer Demand, 1660–1780," in *The Cambridge History of Western Textiles*, ed. David Jenkins (Cambridge: Cambridge University Press, 2003), 1:493–512.

24. Linda Baumgarten, *What Clothes Reveal: The Language of Clothing in Colonial and Federal America* (New Haven: Yale University Press in association with the Colonial Williamsburg Foundation, 2002), 241n43.

25. Lemire, *Fashion's Favourite*, 97–99; John Styles, *The Dress of the People: Everyday Fashion in Eighteenth-Century England* (New Haven: Yale University Press, 2007), 109–32.

26. Beverly Lemire, *Dress, Culture, and Commerce: The English Clothing Trade before the Factory* (Basingstoke: Palgrave Macmillan, 1997), 6.

27. Lemire, *Fashion's Favourite*, 162–65, discusses the relationships between elite and common fashions and how fashionable attire spread through society during the eighteenth century.

28. Lemire, *Dress, Culture and Commerce*, 9–41, explores the importance of ready-made clothes for populations such as the military, slaves, and natives, among others.

29. Pastoureau, *Blue*, 124.

30. In the eighteenth century, cloth merchants increasingly contracted dyers to color material to particular specifications: some of high quality (chiefly for British and European consumption) and a greater amount of lower quality (largely for colonial use). For particulars about one key sector of the British textile industry in the period, wool manufacture, see Smail, *Merchants, Markets, and Manufacture.*

31. A photograph of the swatch and information about the foundling's dress appear in Styles, *Dress of the People*, 115.

32. *Middlesex Journal; or, Chronicle of Liberty*, August 1, 1771.

33. Kathleen Staples, "'Useful, Ornamental, or Necessary in This Province': The Textile Inventory of John Dart, 1754," *Journal of Early Southern Decorative Arts* 29, no. 2 (2003): 39–82; Jelatis, "Tangled Up in Blue," 200.

34. "An Act for the Better Ordering and Governing Negroes and other Slaves," *The Statutes at Large of South Carolina*, ed. David J. McCord (Columbia, S.C.: Johnston, 1840), 7:396, quoted in Staples, "'Useful, Ornamental, or Necessary,'" 59.

35. William L. McDowell Jr., ed., *Colonial Records of South Carolina: Documents Relating to Indian Affairs, May 21, 1750–August 7, 1754* (Columbia: South Carolina Archives Department, 1958), 146–47, quoted in Staples, "'Useful, Ornamental, or Necessary,'" 67–69.

CHAPTER 2. *South Carolina Indigo in the Dress of Slaves and Sovereign Indians*

1. William Blake, *Group of Negros, as Imported to Be Sold for Slaves*, from John Stedman, *Narrative of a Five-Year Expedition against the Revolted Negroes of Surinam, 1772–77* (London, 1796).

2. Henry Timberlake quoted in Duane King, Ken Blankenship, and Barbara Duncan, *Emissaries of Peace: The 1762 Cherokee and British Delegations* (Cherokee, N.C.: Museum of the Cherokee Indian, 2006), 25.

3. Christopher L. Miller and George R. Hamell, "A New Perspective on Indian-White Contact: Cultural Symbols and Colonial Trade," *Journal of American History* 73, no. 2 (1986): 312.

4. For a discussion of how the concept of the fetish developed in relation to trade and conquest in Africa, see Ann Rosalind Jones and Peter Stallybrass, *Renaissance Clothing and the Materials of Memory* (Cambridge: Cambridge University Press, 2000), 10. For an overview of how the concept of the fetish emerged out of colonialism, see William Pietz, "The Problem of the Fetish, I," *Res* 9 (1985): 5–17; William Pietz, "The Problem of the Fetish, II," *Res* 13 (1987): 23–45; William Pietz, "The Problem of the Fetish, IIIa," *Res* 16 (1988): 105–23.

5. Jones and Stallybrass, *Renaissance Clothing*, 10–11. See also William Pietz, "Fetishism and Materialism: The Limits of Theory in Marx," in *Fetishism as Cultural Discourse*, ed. Emily Apter and William Pietz (Ithaca: Cornell University Press, 1993), 119–51.

6. Robert Ross, *Clothing: A Global History* (Cambridge: Polity, 2008), 23–24.

7. Ibid., 25.

8. Philip D. Morgan, *Slave Counterpoint: Black Culture in the Eighteenth-Century Chesapeake and Lowcountry* (Chapel Hill: University of North Carolina Press for the Omohundro Institute of Early American History and Culture, 1998), 131–32, 385, 470.

9. James H. Merrell, *The Indians' New World: Catawbas and Their Neighbors from European Contact through the Era of Removal* (Chapel Hill: University of North Carolina Press for the Omohundro Institute of Early American History and Culture, 1989), 32.

10. Beverly Lemire, *Fashion's Favourite: The Cotton Trade and the Consumer in Britain, 1660–1800* (Oxford: Oxford University Press for the Pasold Research Fund, 1991), 8–13.

11. Beverly Lemire, *Dress, Culture, and Commerce: The English Clothing Trade before the Factory* (Basingstoke: Palgrave Macmillan, 1997), 7.

12. Ibid.

13. Jones and Stallybrass, *Renaissance Clothing*, 11.

14. Morgan, *Slave Counterpoint*, 126.

15. Ibid., 129.

16. Ibid., 127.

17. Ibid., 129.

18. Ibid., 127–28; Kathleen Staples, "'Useful, Ornamental or Necessary in This Province': The Textile Inventory of John Dart, 1754," *Journal of Early Southern Decorative Arts* 29, no. 2 (2003): 61.

19. For an overview of southeastern American Indian dress, see Josephine Paterek, *Encyclopedia of American Indian Costume* (Denver: ABC-CLIO, 1994), 6–8; for the dress of specific Indian groups from the region, see 8–37.

20. Kathryn E. Holland Braund, a specialist on Creek dress and trade, argues that "new European textiles and decorations revolutionized Creek dress" (*Deerskins and Duffels: The Creek Indian Trade with Anglo-America, 1685–1815* [Lincoln: University of Nebraska Press, 1993], 124). While it is true that new materials bred new forms and uses for cloth and fittings, these changes were in keeping with an Indian focus on utility (clothing that provided protection and ease of motion) and sartorial display (as a means of communicating standing and position).

21. Miller and Hamell, "New Perspective," 324–25.

22. For a discussion of the importance of luster to Native Americans, see ibid., 316–17.

23. For a discussion of how blue may have referred to the liminal world of the spirit, see Cory Carole Silverstein, "Clothed Encounters: The Power of Dress in Relations between Anishnaabe and British Peoples in the Great Lakes Region, 1760–2000" (PhD diss., McMaster University, 2000), 203–5.

24. J. T. Garrett, *The Cherokee Herbal: Native Plant Medicine from the Four Directions* (Rochester, Vt.: Bear, 2003), 9.

25. Ibid., 23–24.

26. Ibid., 204.

27. James Mooney reports that with respect to shamanistic practices, blue was traditionally associated with defeat and trouble in Cherokee color symbolism (*Cherokee History, Myths and Sacred Formulas* [1891, 1900; Cherokee, N.C.: Cherokee Publications in collaboration with the Museum of the Cherokee Indian and Qualla Arts and Crafts Mutual, 2006], 342).

28. Braund notes that for Indians, "diplomatic gift exchanges symbolized the ritual joining of the two parties and were an affirmation of faith in the continuance of the relationship" (*Deerskins and Duffels*, 27).

29. Ostenaco's visage is copied from a painting by Joshua Reynolds, and the other two native faces are merely bland ciphers.

30. Alden T. Vaughan, *Transatlantic Encounters: American Indians in Britain, 1500–1776* (Cambridge: Cambridge University Press, 2006), 168–69, 172.

31. Ibid.; Paterek, *Encyclopedia of American Indian Costume*, 11–15.

32. For shininess in American Indian cosmology, see Miller and Hamell, "New Perspective," 315–17.

33. Linda Baumgarten, *What Clothes Reveal: The Language of Clothing in Colonial and Federal America* (New Haven: Yale University Press in association with the Colonial Williamsburg Foundation, 2002), 66–69, 72–74.

34. Reproductions of the portraits appear in King, Blankenship, and Duncan, *Emissaries of Peace*, 54, 56; a color reproduction of the Reynolds portrait appears on the cover of the *Journal of Cherokee Studies* 2, no. 3 (1977).

35. Helen Bradley Foster, *New Raiments of Self: African American Clothing in the Antebellum South* (Oxford: Berg, 1997), 69–70.

36. Linda France Stine, Melanie A. Cabak, and Mark D. Groover, "Blue Beads as African-American Cultural Symbols," *Historical Archaeology* 30, no. 3 (1996): 53.

37. Foster, *New Raiments of Self*, 22. Foster also notes that any emphasis on Arabs introducing clothing to black Africans is ethnocentric; African indigenous dress included coverings of skins, which are certainly a form of dress.

38. Ibid., 34–35.

39. *Captive Passage: The Transatlantic Slave Trade and the Making of the Americas* (Washington: Smithsonian Institution Press in association with the Mariners' Museum, 2002), 22.

40. Foster, *New Raiments of Self*, 62–63.

41. Marietta B. Joseph, "West African Indigo Cloth," *African Arts* 11, no. 2 (1978): 34–35.

42. Foster, *New Raiments of Self*, 57.

43. Stine, Cabak, and Groover, "Blue Beads," 54.

44. Ibid., 62–63.

45. Ibid., 63–64.

46. Roger Pinckney, *Blue Roots: African American Folk Magic of the Gullah People* (Orangeburg, S.C.: Sandlapper, 2003); Juliann Vachon, "Quintessentially Lowcountry: The Meaning of Blue Paint Remains Misty," *Beaufort Gazette*, February 5, 2010, accessed June 23, 2011, http://www.islandpacket.com/2010/02/05/1127632/quintessentially-lowcountry-the.html.

47. Foster, *New Raiments of Self*, 187.

48. Susan P. Shames has recently identified the artist as John Rose (Eve M. Kahn, "'Plantation' Artist Named," *New York Times*, February 10, 2011, accessed June 23, 2011, http://www.nytimes.com/2011/02/11/arts/design/11antiques.html?_r=2&ref=design).

49. Virginia Jelatis, "Tangled Up in Blue: Indigo Culture and Economy in South Carolina, 1747–1800" (PhD diss., University of Minnesota, 1999), 169–72; Baumgarten, *What Clothes Reveal*, 84.

50. Foster, *New Raiments of Self*, 275–81.

51. *South Carolina and American General Gazette*, December 5–11, 1770.

52. Baumgarten, *What Clothes Reveal*, 136.

53. The baldric, now in the collection of Scotland's University of Aberdeen, is reproduced in Susan C. Power, *Art of the Cherokee: Prehistory to the Present* (Athens: University of Georgia Press, 2007), 59.

54. Ibid., 60.

55. Sarah H. Hill, *Weaving New Worlds: Southeastern Cherokee Women and Their Basketry* (Chapel Hill: University of North Carolina Press, 1997), 24.

CHAPTER 3. *Botanists, Merchants, and Planters in South Carolina*

1. Virginia Jelatis, "Tangled Up in Blue: Indigo Culture and Economy in South Carolina, 1747–1800" (PhD diss., University of Minnesota, 1999), 17–18.

2. Ibid., 23–41; David L. Coon, "Eliza Lucas Pinckney and the Reintroduction of Indigo Culture in South Carolina," *Journal of Southern History* 42, no. 1 (1976): 63–65.

3. Jelatis, "Tangled Up in Blue," 197–201.

4. Edmund Berkeley and Dorothy Smith Berkeley, *Dr. Alexander Garden of Charles Town* (Chapel Hill: University of North Carolina Press, 1969); Susan Scott Parrish, *American Curiosity: Cultures of Natural History in the Colonial British Atlantic World* (Chapel Hill: University of North Carolina Press for the Omohundro Institute of Early American History and Culture, 2006), 116–18, 127–34, 235–36, 253, 272–74.

5. Garden was also extremely interested in fauna and sent many animal specimens to collectors in Britain and Europe. See Berkeley and Berkeley, *Dr. Alexander Garden*, appendixes, 341–48.

6. For Garden's relationship with Linnaeus, see Margaret Denny, "Linnaeus and His Disciple in Carolina: Alexander Garden," *Isis* 38, no. 3–4 (1948): 161–74. For the relationship of Linnaeus's endeavor to colonialism, see Staffan Müller-Wille, "Walnuts at Hudson Bay, Coral Reefs in Gotland: The Colonialism of Linnaean Botany," in *Colonial Botany: Science, Commerce, and Politics in the Early Modern World*, ed. Londa Schiebinger and Claudia Swan (Philadelphia: University of Pennsylvania Press, 2005), 34–48. Garden's ambition, the size of the network to which he contributed, and the stature of those who existed at the top of this network underscore the significance of natural history and specifically botany as intellectual pursuits in the eighteenth century.

7. Berkeley and Berkeley, *Dr. Alexander Garden*, 99–103.

8. Ibid., *Dr. Alexander Garden*, 34, 96.

9. H. Baker, F.R.S., "The Effects of the Opuntia, or Prickly Pear, and of the Indigo Plant, in Colouring the Juices of Living Animals," *Philosophical Transactions of the Royal Society* 50 (1757–58): 296–97.

10. The formal, scientific language Garden used to describe his findings about the prickly pear to colleagues at the revered Royal Society contrasts with the informal, rhapsodic words he wrote to a friend in 1756 after learning that he could botanize while traveling with South Carolina governor James Glen to Cherokee Country. In this instance, he effused about what he would surely discover in the mountainous backcountry and how

he was driven by "Sacred thirst" (Berkeley and Berkeley, *Dr. Alexander Garden*, 88). When he sent a fellow botanist a sample of flowers used by the Cherokees to produce red dye, Garden mocked rather than celebrated the spirit: he criticized the Cherokee woman from whom he obtained the plant for assuming that the flower would lose its power when it crossed the ocean to London (Parrish, *American Curiosity*, 235). Like many of his confreres, Garden had room only for his own understanding of the divine, which was mediated by the science he produced to establish godlike stature for himself among fellow enthusiasts.

11. Thomas Hallock describes John Bartram as "the preeminent botanist of the time" (*From the Fallen Tree: Frontier Narratives, Environmental Politics, and the Roots of a National Pastoral, 1749–1826* [Chapel Hill: University of North Carolina Press, 2005], 31).

12. Berkeley and Berkeley, *Dr. Alexander Garden*, 199–205.

13. Ibid., 211–12.

14. Henry Laurens to John Bartram, August 9, 1766, in *The Papers of Henry Laurens*, vol. 5, September 1, 1765–July 31, 1768, ed. David R. Chesnutt (Columbia: University of South Carolina Press, 1974), 151–55.

15. Hallock, *From the Fallen Tree*, 169, notes that Bartram's enthusiasm for the land and native peoples he encountered collided with his interest in seeing that land cultivated by settlers.

16. Ibid., 151.

17. Bartram singled out the Alachua savanna for special attention, noting that it was "very Good & extremely proper for Indigo" (*William Bartram on the Southeastern Indians*, ed. Gregory A. Waselkov and Kathryn E. Holland Braund [Lincoln: University of Nebraska Press, 1995], 243n44).

18. Max S. Edelson maintains that the "Bartrams believed their own hype," since William took up (and failed at) indigo planting in East Florida (*Plantation Enterprise in Colonial South Carolina* [Cambridge: Harvard University Press, 2006], 195).

19. For an overview of indigo production in East Florida, see Joyce E. Chaplin, *An Anxious Pursuit: Agricultural Innovation and Modernity in the Lower South, 1730–1815* (Chapel Hill: University of North Carolina Press for the Omohundro Institute of Early American History and Culture, 1993), 202–20. For a detailed discussion of indigo growing at an important East Florida indigo plantation, see "Indigo Cultivation: Life at Governor James Grant's Villa Plantation," Florida History Online, accessed June 28, 2011, http://www.unf.edu/floridahistoryonline/Plantations/plantations/Indigo_Cultivation_and_Processing.htm.

20. Coon, "Eliza Lucas Pinckney," 71.

21. Barnett A. Elzas, *The Jews of South Carolina: From the Earliest Times to the Present Day* (Philadelphia: Lippincott, 1905), 59–62.

22. R. C. Nash, "The Organization of Trade and Finance in the Atlantic Economy: Britain and South Carolina, 1670–1775," in *Money, Trade, and Power: The Evolution of Colonial South Carolina's Plantation Society*, ed. Jack P. Greene, Rosemary Brana-Shute, and Randy J. Sparks (Columbia: University of South Carolina Press, 2001), 91.

23. Coon, "Eliza Lucas Pinckney," 73–74.

24. James Crokatt, *Further Observations Intended for Improving the Culture and Curing of Indigo, Etc. in South Carolina* (London, 1747) in *The Colonial South Carolina Scene: Contemporary Views, 1697–1774*, ed. H. Roy Merrens (Columbia: University of South Carolina Press, 1977), 149–50.

25. Ibid., 151.

26. Elzas, *Jews of South Carolina*, 48–49.

27. Ibid., 59.

28. Berkeley and Berkeley, *Dr. Alexander Garden*, 119–21.

29. Ibid., 200. For a description of the garden, see Edelson, *Plantation Enterprise*, 225–27.

30. For details on Laurens's plantations and their productivity, see Edelson, *Plantation Enterprise*, 284–86.

31. Ibid., 284, 213.

32. Leila Sellers, *Charleston Business on the Eve of the American Revolution* (Chapel Hill: University of North Carolina Press, 1934), 162; Edelson, *Plantation Enterprise*, 247.

33. Berkeley and Berkeley, *Dr. Alexander Garden*, 165–66, 254–56.

34. J. Russell Snapp, *John Stuart and the Struggle for Empire on the Southern Frontier* (Baton Rouge: Louisiana State University Press, 1996), 47.

35. Berkeley and Berkeley, *Dr. Alexander Garden*, 254.

36. Ibid., 256. For a description of George Ogilvie's challenges with his South Carolina property and the charm of Garden's Otranto, see George Ogilvie and Alexander Garden, "Appendix: The Letters of George Ogilvie," *Southern Literary Journal* 18, George Ogilvie's Narrative Poem "Carolina; or, The Planter" (1986): 117–34.

37. Berkeley and Berkeley, *Dr. Alexander Garden*, 249.

38. Edelson, *Plantation Enterprise*, 145.

39. Berkeley and Berkeley, *Dr. Alexander Garden*, 272, 273.

40. Ibid., 276.

41. Ibid., 275.

42. For a description of how planters saw their plantations as "arcadian retreat[s]," see Edelson, *Plantation Enterprise*, 209–10.

43. Hennig Cohen, "A Colonial Poem on Indigo Culture," *Agricultural History* 30, no. 1 (1956): 41.

44. Woodmason arrived in Charles Town in 1752 and became a planter in the Peedee River area. In addition to his illustrated essay on indigo manufacture (Charles Woodmason, "The Indigo Plant Described," *Gentleman's Magazine and Historical Quarterly* 25 [1755]: 201–3), he published a poem on Benjamin Franklin (with an imitation of Horace over his initials) and Greco-Roman style poetry on South Carolina land and its planters (see Claude E. Jones, "Charles Woodmason as a Poet," *South Carolina Historical Magazine* 59, no. 4 [1958]: 189–94). The style of his poetry and his knowledge of indigo make him a strong candidate as author of the poem on indigo.

45. Coon, "Eliza Lucas Pinckney," 73.

46. Ibid., 72, 75.

47. The book in which the poem was meant to appear was never published (Cohen, "Colonial Poem," 44).

48. The text is reproduced in *Colonial South Carolina Scene*, ed. Merrens, 160–63; the woodcut is reproduced in Chaplin, *Anxious Pursuit*, 196.

49. Jones, "Charles Woodmason as a Poet," 189.

50. Cohen, "Colonial Poem," 41.

51. Ibid., 42–44.

52. Ibid., 43–44. Cohen does not explicitly identify Pinckney as the writer who applauded the poem's usefulness but instead lists Agricola, Pinckney's pseudonym.

53. Edelson, *Plantation Enterprise*, 209–10.

54. Berkeley and Berkeley, *Dr. Alexander Garden*, 352, 354.

55. Ibid., 236.

CHAPTER 4. *The Role of Indigo in Native-Colonist Struggles over Land and Goods*

1. William L. McDowell Jr., ed., *Documents Relating to Indian Affairs, 1754–1765* (Columbia: University of South Carolina Press for the South Carolina Department of Archives and History, 1970), 115.

2. Robert L. Meriwether, *The Expansion of South Carolina, 1729–1765* (Philadelphia: Porcupine, 1974), 167.

3. Stephen J. Hornsby, *British Atlantic, American Frontier: Spaces of Power in Early Modern British America* (Hanover: University Press of New England, 2005), 112.

4. J. Leitch Wright Jr., *The Only Land They Knew: The Tragic Story of the American Indians in the Old South* (New York: Free Press, 1981), 22–26, 217–18; Robert M. Weir, *Colonial South Carolina: A History* (Columbia: University of South Carolina Press, 1983), 11–12; Paul Kelton, *Epidemics and Enslavement: Biological Catastrophe in the Native Southeast, 1492–1715* (Lincoln: University of Nebraska Press, 2007).

5. James H. Merrell, *The Indians' New World: Catawbas and Their Neighbors from European Contact through the Era of Removal* (Chapel Hill: University of North Carolina Press for the Institute of Early American History and Culture, 1989), 95–99.

6. Bert W. Bierer, *South Carolina Indian Lore* (Columbia: Bierer, 1972), 10–14.

7. Hornsby, *British Atlantic, American Frontier*, 114. Hornsby also notes that in 1708, about one-third of the South Carolina colony's forty-three hundred slaves were Indian. Weir maintains that "South Carolinians were *the* Indian slave traders of the North American continent. In fact, so many Indian slaves were exported from the colony that in 1715 Connecticut and some of the other New England colonies specifically barred their importation from Carolina" (*Colonial South Carolina*, 26).

8. J. Russell Snapp, *John Stuart and the Struggle for Empire on the Southern Frontier* (Baton Rouge: Louisiana State University Press, 1996), 11.

9. Gary L. Hewitt, "The State in the Planters' Service: Politics and the Emergence of a Plantation Economy in South Carolina," in *Money, Trade, and Power: The Evolution of Colonial South Carolina's Plantation Economy*, ed. Jack P. Greene, Rosemary Brana-Shute, and Randy J. Sparks (Columbia: University of South Carolina Press, 2001), 50–51. Hewitt notes that "from the beginning of colonial settlement in 1670, South Carolina's trade with its Indian neighbors had been the most dynamic sector of the colonial economy and a central part of the colony's diplomatic relationships with its neighbors" (51).

10. Ibid., 50.

11. Walter Edgar, *South Carolina: A History* (Columbia: University of South Carolina Press, 1998), 154.

12. Hewitt, "State in the Planters' Service," 57. Snapp notes that the Yamassee and their allies destroyed "over four hundred lives and property worth £400,000" (*John Stuart*, 15).

13. Hewitt, "State in the Planters' Service," 57.

14. Ibid., 52–53.

15. Ibid., 54–55.

16. Ibid., 58.

17. Ibid., 51.

18. Ibid., 56–57.

19. Wesley White has done extensive research to document in text and maps the area set aside for the Peedees and Natchez. Until 1737, the Peedees had lived on the Great Peedee River, but around that time, they acquired a one-hundred-acre reservation with the Natchez on Edisto River's Indian Field Swamp. Between 1740 and 1742, the Peedees appeared to have left the reservation to settle in part at Four Hole Swamp and in part on the Santee River. For the particulars of the transactions involved, see extract from *Charleston Deeds*, Book S, 190–92, Wesley D. White Papers, 1521–1993 (1311.00), South

Carolina Historical Society, Charleston. For the creation of the Catawba reservation, see Merrell, *Indians' New World*, 198–203.

20. Hewitt, "State in the Planters' Service," 66–67.

21. For figures on South Carolina rice production and how it intertwined with increasing slave numbers, see Weir, *Colonial South Carolina*, 145–46.

22. Hewitt, "State in the Planters' Service," 51.

23. Edgar, *South Carolina*, 69.

24. Virginia Jelatis, "Tangled Up in Blue: Indigo Culture and Economy in South Carolina, 1747–1800" (PhD diss., University of Minnesota, 1999), 103.

25. Like the South Carolina township scheme, "Georgia promised better security on the southern frontier" (Weir, *Colonial South Carolina*), 113.

26. Rachel N. Klein, *Unification of a Slave State: The Rise of the Planter Class in the South Carolina Backcountry* (Chapel Hill: University of North Carolina Press for the Institute of Early American History and Culture, 1990), 14–15.

27. Ibid., 11–15.

28. In the White Papers, the details of this transaction are cited as "*Council Journal*, British Public Records Office Photostat 2, June 8 and 15, South Carolina Archives; *Colonial Plats*, vol. 2, 430 and vol. 4, 229, South Carolina Archives."

29. See s213184: *Colonial Plat Books*, John Newberry Plat for 350 acres in Welch Tract, 9/2/1738, South Carolina Department of History and Archives Online Database, accessed June 30, 2011, http://www.archivesindex.sc.gov/onlinearchives/Thumbnails.aspx?recordId=94704.

30. Meriwether, *Expansion of South Carolina*, 93.

31. Jelatis, "Tangled Up in Blue," 140.

32. Meriwether, *Expansion of South Carolina*, 167.

33. The Southern backcountry included the Piedmont regions of Maryland, Virginia, the Carolinas, and Georgia as well as the Great Valley from southern Pennsylvania through western Virginia to the Carolinas and Georgia. By the middle of the eighteenth century, it was the "most dynamic agricultural frontier in colonial British America" (Hornsby, *British Atlantic, American Frontier*, 164–65).

34. Klein, *Unification of a Slave State*, 16.

35. The available documents do not establish all of the backcountry areas in which indigo was grown or name all of those who grew it (ibid., 21n21).

36. Jelatis, "Tangled Up in Blue," 124–26.

37. Klein, *Unification of a Slave State*, 20.

38. Snapp, *John Stuart*, 21–22.

39. Extract from *Charleston Deeds*, Book S, 190–92, White Papers.

40. Planter William Henry Drayton, through his grandfather, South Carolina governor William Bull, got private leave of the Catawba reservation: Drayton offered natives protection from squatters and payments in trade goods including matchcoats; however, he planned to settle their lands. The Indians did not understand Drayton's intentions, but Indian commissioner John Stuart saw Drayton's dealings as a means of cheating the Catawbas and convinced the South Carolina Council to rescind its arrangement with Drayton (Snapp, *John Stuart*, 149–51).

41. In the White Papers, the details of this transaction are cited as "*Council Journal*, no. 11, July 25, 1744, 423–17."

42. William L. McDowell Jr., ed., *Documents Relating to Indian Affairs, May 21, 1750–August 7, 1754* (Columbia: South Carolina Archives Department, 1958), 376.

43. In the White Papers, the details of this transaction are cited as "*Council Journal*, Sainsbury Copy, numbered from pages 293 to 648, South Carolina Archives, 327–28."

44. Bernard Vincent, "Slaveholding Indians: The Case of the Cherokee Nation," *DEP* 5–6 (2006): 5.

45. Snapp, *John Stuart*, 86.

46. Kelton, *Epidemics and Enslavement*, 218.

47. McDowell, *Documents Relating to Indian Affairs, May 21, 1750–August 7, 1754*, 407.

48. See *Journal of Cherokee Studies* 2, no. 3 (1977).

49. McDowell, *Documents Relating to Indian Affairs, 1754–1765*, 535.

50. Kathryn E. Holland Braund, *Deerskin and Duffels: The Creek Indian Trade with Anglo-America, 1685–1815* (Lincoln: University of Nebraska Press, 1993), 122.

51. Snapp, *John Stuart*, 33–34.

52. Ibid., 38–39.

53. Ibid., 39.

54. Ibid., 43.

55. Hornsby, *British Atlantic, American Frontier*, 117. Notable among these reports was one by the South Carolina governor. See James Glen, *A Description of South Carolina: Containing Many Curious and Interesting Particulars Relating to the Civil, Natural, and Commercial History* (London, 1761), 9–10.

56. Joyce E. Chaplin, *An Anxious Pursuit: Agricultural Innovation and Modernity in the Lower South, 1730–1815* (Chapel Hill: University of North Carolina Press for the Institute of Early American History and Culture, 1993), 208.

57. Snapp, *John Stuart*, 43.

58. Ibid., 117.

59. Quoted in ibid., 119.

60. Ibid., 137, 135.

61. Hewitt, "State in the Planters' Service," 55.

CHAPTER 5. *Producing South Carolina Indigo*

1. *South Carolina and American General Gazette*, January 21, 1779, cited in Wesley D. White Papers, 1521–1993 (1311.00), South Carolina Historical Society, Charleston.

2. Philip D. Morgan, *Slave Counterpoint: Black Culture in the Eighteenth-Century Chesapeake and Lowcountry* (Chapel Hill: University of North Carolina Press for the Omohundro Institute of Early American History and Culture, 1998), 598–99.

3. Ibid., 481.

4. For powerful documentation of this fact, see the White Papers.

5. William Robert Snell, "Indian Slavery in South Carolina, 1671–1795" (PhD diss., University of Alabama, 1972), chaps. 1–3, appendix 5, 150–60.

6. See the White Papers.

7. Edward Reynolds, "Human Commerce," in *Captive Passage: The Transatlantic Slave Trade and the Making of the Americas* (Washington, D.C.: Smithsonian Institution Press in association with the Mariners' Museum, 2002), 13–33.

8. Snell, "Indian Slavery."

9. Ibid., chaps. 1, 2.

10. Ibid., 35; Paul Kelton, *Epidemics and Enslavement: Biological Catastrophe in the Native Southeast, 1492–1715* (Lincoln: University of Nebraska Press, 2007), 103–4.

11. Snell, "Indian Slavery," appendix I, 125–32.

12. Kelton, *Epidemics and Enslavement*, 103–4.

13. Snell, "Indian Slavery," chap. 4.

14. Morgan, *Slave Counterpoint*, 1.

15. Snell, "Indian Slavery," appendix IV; Peter H. Wood, *Black Majority: Negroes in Colonial South Carolina from 1670 through the Stono Rebellion* (New York: Knopf, 1974); Judith A. Carney, *Black Rice: The African Origins of Rice Cultivation in the Americas* (Cambridge: Harvard University Press, 2001).

16. Snell, "Indian Slavery," 116.

17. Morgan, *Slave Counterpoint*, 482.

18. Ibid.

19. Ibid., 477–85; Theda Purdue, *"Mixed Blood" Indians: Racial Construction in the Early South* (Athens: University of Georgia Press, 2003), 5–6; Eiryls M. Barker, "Indian Traders, Charles Town, and London's Vital Links to the Interior of North America," in *Money, Trade, and Power: The Evolution of Colonial South Carolina's Plantation Society*, ed. Jack P.

Greene, Rosemary Brana-Shute, and Randy J. Sparks (Columbia: University of South Carolina Press, 2001), 151.

20. Michael J. Heitzler, *Goose Creek: A Definitive History*, vol. 1, *Planters, Politicians, and Patriots* (Charleston, S.C.: History Press, 2005), 88; Morgan, *Slave Counterpoint*, 482n71.

21. Kathryn E. Holland Braund, "The Creek Indians, Blacks, and Slavery," *Journal of Southern History* 57, no. 4 (1991): 617.

22. Claudio Saunt, "'The English Has Now a Mind to Make Slaves of Them All': Creeks, Seminoles, and the Problem of Slavery," *American Indian Quarterly* 22, no. 1–2 (1998): 165.

23. Max S. Edelson, *Plantation Enterprise in Colonial South Carolina* (Cambridge: Harvard University Press, 2006), 184.

24. Coon, "Eliza Lucas Pinckney," 71–72.

25. Elias Monnereau, *The Complete Indigo-Maker, Containing an Accurate Account of the Indigo Plant; Its Description, Culture, Preparation, and Manufacture with Œconomical Rules and Necessary Directions for a Planter How to Manage a Plantation, and Employ His Negroes to the Best Advantage, to Which Is Added, a Treatise on the Culture of Coffee* (London, 1769), 50.

26. Frederick C. Knight, *Working the Diaspora: The Impact of African Labor on the Anglo-American World, 1650–1850* (New York: New York University Press, 2010), 93–94.

27. Ibid., 97.

28. Ibid., 100.

29. For the mixed blessings Eliza Lucas Pinckney received from the first Montserrat dye maker with whom she worked, see Coon, "Eliza Lucas Pinckney," 66.

30. Virginia Gail Jelatis, "Tangled Up in Blue: Indigo Culture and Economy in South Carolina, 1747–1800" (PhD diss., University of Minnesota, 1999), 152–53; Knight, *Working the Diaspora*, 104–8.

31. Charles Spencer, *Edisto Island, 1663 to 1860: Wild Eden to Cotton Aristocracy* (Charleston, S.C.: History Press, 2008), 69. See also Julie Dash's 1991 film, *Daughters of the Dust*, which shows slaves dyeing material in such pits.

32. Kate P. Kent, review of *Into Indigo: African Textiles and Dyeing Techniques*, by Claire Polakoff, *African Arts* 14, no. 1 (1980): 28.

33. Duncan Clarke, "West African Indigo: An Introduction," Adire African Textiles, February 13, 2010, accessed July 8, 2001, http://adireafricantextiles.blogspot.com/2010/02/indigo-in-west-africa-introduction.html.

34. Other examples have also been found: a tabby vat on Port Royal Island and a set of brick vats on Johns Island (Ralph Bailey Jr. to author, November 14, 2012).

35. For an evocative description of this labor gleaned in part from planters' accounts, see Edelson, *Plantation Enterprise*, 159–60.

36. Morgan, *Slave Counterpoint*, 160.

37. Ibid., 164.

38. David B. Schneider, "Otranto Plantation Indigo Vats," U.S. Department of the Interior, National Parks Service, National Register of Historic Places Registration Form, March 25, 1988, accessed July 8, 2011, http://www.nationalregister.sc.gov/berkeley/S10817708012/S10817708012.pdf.

39. Morgan, *Slave Counterpoint*, 163; William S. Coker, "Spanish Regulation of the Natchez Indigo Industry, 1793–1794: The South's First Antipollution Laws?," *Technology and Culture* 13, no. 1 (1972): 55–58.

40. Snell, "Indian Slavery," 150. His appendix V (150–60) provides details of Indian and black slaves' employ gleaned from a variety of colonial records.

41. Morgan, *Slave Counterpoint*, 348–53, discusses this matter as well as some slave artisans' ability to hire themselves out.

42. For relevant and extensive documentation, see the White Papers.

43. David Hancock, *Citizens of the World: London Merchants and the Integration of the British Atlantic Community* (Cambridge: Cambridge University Press, 1995), 167.

CHAPTER 6. *Indigo and an East Florida Plantation*

1. David Hancock, *Citizens of the World: London Merchants and the Integration of the British Atlantic Community, 1735–1785* (Cambridge: Cambridge University Press), 167–68.

2. Ibid.

3. Eirlys Mair Baker, "'Much Blood and Treasure': South Carolina's Indian Traders, 1670–1755" (PhD diss., College of William and Mary, 1993), 80–81.

4. Lewis C. Gray, *History of Agriculture in the Southern United States to 1860* (1933; Gloucester, Mass.: Smith, 1958), 129.

5. Philip M. Brown, "Early Indian Trade in the Development of South Carolina: Politics, Economics, and Social Mobility during the Proprietary Period, 1670–1719," *South Carolina Historical Magazine* 76, no. 3 (1975): 118.

6. S. Max Edelson, *Plantation Enterprise in Colonial South Carolina* (Cambridge: Harvard University Press, 2006), 203–6.

7. Ibid., 192–93.

8. Henry Laurens, *The Papers of Henry Laurens*, vol. 4, September 1, 1763–August 31, 1765, ed. George C. Rogers Jr. (Columbia: University of South Carolina Press, 1974), 337–38.

9. Edelson, *Plantation Enterprise*, 205.

10. J. Russell Snapp, *John Stuart and the Struggle for Empire on the Southern Frontier* (Baton Rouge: Louisiana State University Press, 1996), 79.

11. Edelson, *Plantation Enterprise*, 214–18.

12. Laurens, *Papers of Henry Laurens*, 4:117, 464, 337.

13. Virginia Gail Jelatis, "Tangled Up in Blue: Indigo Culture and Economy in South Carolina, 1747–1800 (PhD diss., University of Minnesota, 1999), 124–28, 138–41.

14. Hancock, *Citizens of the World*, 157–59.

15. Ibid., 159.

16. Ibid., 151–53.

17. Laurens, *Papers of Henry Laurens*, 4:585.

18. Daniel L. Schafer, "A Swamp of an Investment?: Richard Oswald's East Florida Plantation Experiment," in *Colonial Plantations and Economy in Florida*, ed. Jane G. Landers (Gainesville: University Press of Florida, 2000), 17.

19. Hancock, *Citizens of the World*, 167.

20. Henry Laurens, *The Papers of Henry Laurens*, vol. 5, September 1, 1765–July 31, 1768, ed. George C. Rogers Jr. (Columbia: University of South Carolina Press, 1976), 227.

21. Rachel N. Klein, *Unification of a Slave State: The Rise of the Planter Class in the South Carolina Backcountry, 1760–1808* (Chapel Hill: University of North Carolina University Press for the Institute of Early American Culture and History, 1990), 62–63.

22. See, for example, Laurens, *Papers of Henry Laurens*, 5:22n8.

23. Henry Laurens, *The Papers of Henry Laurens*, vol. 3, January 1, 1759–August 31, 1763, ed. George C. Rogers Jr. (Columbia: University of South Carolina Press, 1972), 75.

24. Ibid., 279.

25. Tom Hatley, *The Dividing Paths: Cherokees and South Carolinians through the Era of Revolution* (New York: Oxford University Press, 1993), 144–45.

26. Laurens, *Papers of Henry Laurens*, 3:284.

27. William Kauffman Scarborough, "The Southern Plantation Overseer: A Re-Evaluation," *Agricultural History* 38, no. 1 (1964): 13–20.

28. Chapman J. Milling, *Red Carolinians* (Columbia: University of South Carolina Press, 1969), 62.

29. Kathryn E. Holland Braund, *Deerskins and Duffels: The Creek Indian Trade with Anglo-America, 1685–1815* (Lincoln: University of Nebraska Press, 1993), 46, 21; Larry Koger, *Black Slaveowners: Free Black Slave Masters in South Carolina, 1790–1860* (Columbia: University of South Carolina Press, 1985), 40.

30. Hancock, *Citizens of the World*, 167–68.

31. Schafer, "Swamp of an Investment?," 18.

32. "Africans in America—Revolution, Part 2, 1750–1805: Fort Mose," PBS, accessed July 12, 2011, http://www.pbs.org/wgbh/aia/part2/2h14.html.

33. "Addison Blockhouse Historic State Park, Bulow Creek State Park, Bulow Plantation Ruins Historic State Park, Tomoko State Park, Multi-Park Unit Management Plan," Florida Department of Environmental Protection, Division of Recreation and

Parks, February 7, 2003, 80, accessed July 12, 2011, http://www.dep.state.fl.us/parks /planning/parkplans/TomokaStatePark.pdf.

34. Gregory A. Waselkov and Kathryn E. Holland Braund, eds., *William Bartram on the Southeastern Indians* (Lincoln: University of Nebraska Press, 1995), 44–45.

CHAPTER 7. *Slave John Williams*

1. This wrap is in the possession of Eliza Lucas Pinckney descendant Tim Drake, who kindly made it available to me for inspection. Another version of material in this chapter appears in Andrea Feeser, "The Exceptional and the Expected: Red, White, and Black Made Blue in Colonial South Carolina," in *The Materiality of Color: The Production, Circulation, and Application of Dyes and Pigments, 1400–1800*, ed. Andrea Feeser, Maureen Daly Goggin, and Beth Fowkes Tobin (Aldershot, Eng.: Ashgate, 2012), 155–66.

2. Susan Scott Parrish, *American Curiosity: Cultures of Natural History in the Colonial British Atlantic World* (Chapel Hill: University of North Carolina Press for the Omohundro Institute of Early American History and Culture, 2006), 205; Eliza Lucas Pinckney, *The Letterbook of Eliza Lucas Pinckney*, ed. Elise Pinckney (Chapel Hill: University of North Carolina Press, 1972), xxiii–iv.

3. As scholars have looked more closely at the history of Eliza Lucas Pinckney and her indigo experiments, they have also retrieved the names of some of the young woman's white helpmates: for example, David L. Coon has highlighted the specific contributions made by her father, George Lucas; her husband, Charles Pinckney; her hired dye makers, Nicholas and Patrick Cromwell; and her neighbor planter, Andrew Deveaux ("Eliza Lucas Pinckney and the Reintroduction of Indigo Culture in South Carolina," *Journal of Southern History* 42, no. 1 [1976]: 61–76).

4. Nicola Phillips, *Women in Business, 1700–1850* (Woodbridge, Eng.: Boydell, 2006); Beverly Lemire, *Dress, Culture, and Commerce: The English Clothing Trade before the Factory, 1660–1800* (Basingstoke: Macmillan, 1997); Mary Ferrari, "'Obliged to Earn Subsistence for Themselves': Women Artisans in Charles Town, South Carolina, 1763–1808," *South Carolina Historical Magazine* 106, no. 4 (2005): 235–51.

5. Pinckney, *Letterbook*, xxiv–xxv.

6. "South Carolina—Indians, Native Americans—Wappoo," South Carolina Information Highway, 2009, accessed July 2, 2009, www.sciway.net/hist/indians/wappoo.html. Any surviving Wappoos were probably absorbed into the mixed population of Settlement Indians (see Chapman J. Milling, *Red Carolinians* [Columbia: University of South Carolina Press, 1969], 62–64).

7. Harriet Simons Williams, "Eliza Lucas and Her Family before the Letterbook," *South Carolina Historical Magazine* 99, no. 3 (1998): 259–79.

8. Ibid.

9. Ibid., 277, 272–74.

10. By 1726, South Carolina planters were required to hire one white man for every ten slaves, although this act was often subverted. See Philip D. Morgan, *Slave Counterpoint: Black Culture in the Eighteenth-Century Chesapeake and Lowcountry* (Chapel Hill: University of North Carolina Press for the Omohundro Institute of Early American History and Culture, 1998), 221.

11. Coon, "Eliza Lucas Pinckney," 69–70.

12. Pinckney, *Letterbook*; *South Carolina Gazette*, June 11, 1744.

13. Edmund Berkeley and Dorothy Smith Berkeley, *Dr. Alexander Garden of Charles Town* (Chapel Hill: University of North Carolina Press, 1969), 34.

14. Pinckney, *Letterbook*, July 1740, 8; Eliza Lucas to George Lucas, June 4, 1741, in Pinckney, *Letterbook*, 16.

15. Williams, "Eliza Lucas," 261.

16. Ibid.

17. Eliza Lucas to Mary Bartlett [1742], in Pinckney, *Letterbook*, 34.

18. Joyce E. Chaplin, *An Anxious Pursuit: Agricultural Innovation and Modernity in the Lower South, 1730–1815* (Chapel Hill: University of North Carolina Press for the Institute of Early American History and Culture, 1993), 85.

19. Morgan, *Slave Counterpoint*, 222.

20. Pinckney, *Letterbook*, January 7, 1742/3, 57.

21. Ibid.

22. "List of Negroes Executed for the Late Conspiracy at Antigua and of Others Banished," May 26, 1737, Board of Trade Original Correspondence, 1737–40, National Archives, Public Records Office, CO 152/23, London.

23. See Pinckney, *Letterbook*, 1740–44, 5–71; Eliza Pinckney to Charles Cotesworth Pinckney, September 10, 1785, Manuscript Collection, Charles Town Library Society, Charles Town, S.C.

24. George Lucas to Charles Pinckney, January 30, 1744, Pinckney Family Papers, Manuscripts Division, Library of Congress.

25. An Act of the Island of Montserrat Entitled an Act for the Further Restriction of Slaves, by Prohibiting Them from Planting Any Indigo, Cotton, Ginger, Coffee, or Cocoa, and from Keeping a Public Market on Sundays and for Further Refraining Licentious Meetings of Negroes, 1737, Board of Trade Original Correspondence.

26. See Pinckney, *Letterbook*, 1740–44, 5–71; Eliza Pinckney to Charles Cotesworth Pinckney, September 10, 1785, Manuscript Collection, Charles Town Library Society.

27. Eliza Pinckney to Charles Cotesworth Pinckney, September 10, 1785, Manuscript Collection, Charles Town Library Society.

28. Ibid.

29. Pinckney, *Letterbook*, xix.

30. George Lucas to Charles Pinckney, 1744, Charleston Archive, Charleston County Public Library, Miscellaneous Records, Charles Town County, 1746–49, Record 75-B, 373–74.

31. Harriott Horry Ravenel, *Eliza Pinckney* (1896; Spartanburg, S.C.: Reprint Company, 1967), 104–5.

32. *South Carolina Gazette*, April 1, 1745.

33. George Lucas to Charles Pinckney [ca. November 1744–May 22, 1745], H. Hyrnes to Charles Pinckney, May 13, 1747, George Lucas to Charles Pinckney, July 12, 1745, all in Pinckney Family Papers.

34. George Lucas to Charles Pinckney, December 24, 1744, ibid.

35. Pinckney, *Letterbook*, xix.

36. Alice R. Smith and D. E. Huger Smith, *The Dwelling Houses of Charles Town, South Carolina* (Philadelphia: Lippincott, 1917), 366.

37. George Lucas to Charles Pinckney, [ca. November 1744–May 22, 1745], Pinckney Family Papers.

38. George Lucas to Charles Pinckney, May 22, 1745, ibid.

39. Smith and Smith, *Dwelling Houses*, 371. That John Williams was extremely knowledgeable about building is further evident from a later entry in Charles Pinckney's account book: Williams bought an architecture book from Pinckney sometime around 1754 (see foldout in the back of the ledger, Pinckney Family Papers).

40. Smith and Smith, *Dwelling Houses*, 367.

41. Ibid, 366.

42. Ibid., 371–72.

43. Andrew Rutledge and William Boone, attorneys for Charles Alexander, to Charles Pinckney, bill of sale for five slaves, January 5, 1750, Miscellaneous Records (Main Series) [Selected Volumes], South Carolina Department of Archives and History, Columbia; Smith and Smith, *Dwelling Houses*, 366.

44. Charles Pinckney, manumission document for John Williams, May 12, 1750, Pinckney Family Papers.

45. A. S. Salley Jr., ed., *Register of St. Philip's Parish, 1720–1758* (Columbia: University of South Carolina Press, n.d.), 137; Charles and Elizabeth Pinckney to Alexander Garden, in trust for John Williams, two subdivisions of four town lots, July 16–17, 1750, in *South Carolina Deed Abstracts, 1719–1772* (Easley, S.C.: Southern Historical, 1984), 2:213.

46. Joseph Pickering to John Williams, receipt for purchase of three slaves, October 14, 1751, Charleston Archive, Charleston County Public Library, record 80A, 105. Williams

purchased Mary and Sabina (here listed as Sabrina) along with Peter, all three of whom were listed as children of Molly, a slave owned by Pickering.

47. John Williams to Benjamin Garden, Sampson Neyle, and Francis Bremar, trustees for Ann Stiles, security on bond, October 23–24, 1758, in *South Carolina Deed Abstracts*, 3:80.

48. *South Carolina Gazette*, August 6, 1763.

49. Charles Pinckney to George Lucas, acceptance of Wappoo Plantation and 20 accompanying slaves as dowry, May 1, 1744, Charleston Archive, Charleston County Public Library, Miscellaneous Records, Charleston County, 1746–49, 375; George Lucas to Charles Alexander, release from mortgages on five plantations, August 25, 1746, Miscellaneous Records (Main Series) [Selected Volumes], South Carolina Department of Archives and History.

50. George Lucas to Charles Alexander, release from mortgages on five plantations, August 25, 1746, Miscellaneous Records (Main Series) [Selected Volumes], South Carolina Department of Archives and History.

51. Andrew Rutledge and William Boone, attorneys for Charles Alexander, to Charles Pinckney, bill of sale for five slaves, January 5, 1750, Miscellaneous Records (Main Series) [Selected Volumes], South Carolina Department of Archives and History.

52. Certificate showing that upon marrying Elizabeth Lucas, Charles Pinckney received from George Lucas the plantation Wappoo and twenty working slaves, May 1, 1744, Miscellaneous Records (Main Series) [Selected Volumes], South Carolina Department of Archives and History. This document also describes Mary Ann (spelled Mariann) as a mulatto.

53. Winthrop D. Jordan, "American Chiaroscuro: The Status and Definition of Mulattoes in the British Colonies," *William and Mary Quarterly* 19, no. 2 (1962): 183–200; Donald L. Horowitz, "Color Differentiation in the American Systems of Slavery," *Journal of Interdisciplinary History* 3, no. 3 (1973): 509–41.

54. Charles Pinckney to George Lucas, acceptance of Wappoo Plantation and 20 accompanying slaves as dowry, May 1, 1744, Charleston Archive, Charleston County Public Library, Miscellaneous Records, Charleston County, 1746–49, 375.

CONCLUSION. *South Carolina Indigo*

1. David N. Carvalho, *Forty Centuries of Ink* (Middlesex, Eng.: Echo, 2007), 101–2.

2. "Laundry Blue," Old and Interesting, accessed July 8, 2011, http://www.oldand interesting.com/laundry-blue.aspx; Theresa Fairbanks Harris and Scott Wilcox, with essays and contributions by Stephen Daniels, Michael Fuller, and Maureen Green,

Papermaking and the Art of Watercolor in Eighteenth-Century Britain: Paul Sanby and the Whatman Paper Mill (New Haven: Yale University Press in association with the Yale Center for British Art, 2006), 84.

3. "South Carolina State Flag," 50States.com, accessed July 8, 2011, http://www.50states.com/flag/scflag.htm.

4. Richard Rogers, "Feeling Blue in South Carolina," HD News 12 WRDW-TV Augusta, March 12, 2008, accessed July 8, 2011, http://www.wrdw.com/home/headlines/16586141.html.

5. For Moultrie's role as a captain under Henry Laurens in the war against the Cherokee, see Tom Hatley, *The Dividing Paths: Cherokees and South Carolinians through the Era of Revolution* (New York: Oxford University Press, 1993), 198. For Moultrie's killing and capture of runaway slaves, see David Lee Russell, *The American Revolution in the Southern Colonies* (Jefferson, N.C.: McFarland, 2000), 309.

INDEX

clothing: baldric, 41–42, 120n53; belt, 33, 37; blanket, 26, 32, 73, 83; cap, 41; cape, 38; coat, 25, 31, 37, 41; dress, 2–5, 40, 109–11, 117n31; flap, 26, 33; gifted, 6, 36; handkerchief, 25–26, 32; headdress, 15, 83; head wrap, 38, 40; jacket, 25, 40–41, 73; leggings, 33, 37; livery, 31–32; mantle, 26, 37; matchcoat, 6, 26, 33, 37, 73, 111, 127n40; moccasins, 41; ready-made, 6, 22–23, 25, 32–33, 41, 117n28; sash, 41; shift, 25, 33; shirt, 23, 25–26, 33, 37; shoes, 32; stockings, 23, 32; trousers, 25, 25, 84; uniform, 1, 23, 31, 111; waistcoat, 27; wrap, 35, 39, 99, 109–110, 132n1. *See also* attire

Congarees, 61, 63

Creeks (American Indians), 31, 61–62, 65, 68–71, 77, 96, 97

Crokatt, James, 50–51, 52, 78, 88, 123n24

Cromwell, Nicholas, 103–5, 132n3

Cromwell, Patrick, 104–5, 132n3

Cunne Shote (Cherokee headman), 36–37

Dart, John, 24–26, 117n33

deerskins, 25–26, 30, 50, 62, 67, 69, 75, 88, 94, 119n20

Deveaux, Andrew, 101, 103, 132n3

driver, 96, 100, 102. *See also* Williams, John

dye, 4, 15, 23, 39, 47, 50, 110, 114n3, 121–22n10. *See also* indigo

dyeing, 1, 15, 110, 116n21

dye maker, 18, 77–79, 82, 103–4, 105, 132n3

dyer, 1, 16–17, 19, 21, 22–24, 31, 114n2, 115n14, 116n21, 117n30. *See also* Ledyard, John

East Florida. *See* Florida

farms, 1, 4, 48, 69; farmers and, 37, 64, 66–67, 70, 94–96; farming and, 64–67, 70, 72, 74, 76, 89, 92, 95–96, 98

fetish: amulet, 28–29, 39; concept, 29, 118n4, 118n5

Florida, 49, 52, 61; as backcountry, 67, 93, 95; British, 48, 70, 91–92; Fort Mose, 97, 131n32; free black communities and, 92, 97; fugitives and, 92–93; Indians (American) and, 7, 67, 72, 87, 96–98; runaway slaves and, 92, 97; Spanish, 62, 97; St. Augustine, 62, 91, 97. *See also under* indigo; Laurens, Henry

France: as Britain's enemy, 48, 55, 62, 64, 66, 72; as indigo producer, 6, 16–21, 23, 50–51, 78, 104

Galphin, George, 76–77, 96

Garden, Alexander: Bartram family and, 48, 53; as

botanist, 46–48, 53–54, 101, 121–22n10; as British Loyalist, 47, 54; and Ellis, John, 51–52; indigo and, 46–48, 52–54, 57, 59–60, 82; Laurens and, 48, 52; Linnaeus and, 46–47, 121n6; as natural scientist, 46, 57, 121n5; and Ogilvie, Charles, 53–54; and Ogilvie, George, 53–54, 57–58, 70, 123n36; Otranto Plantation and, 53–54, 57–58, 80, 82, 123n36; pastoralism and, 54, 57; as physician, 46; and Pinckney, Eliza Lucas, 101; as planter, 46–47, 53–54, 57

Georgia: African American culture and, 39; as backcountry, 52, 67, 93, 126n33; Creeks (American Indians) and, 70–71, 93, 97; escaped slaves and, 97; fugitives and, 92; plantations and, 72, 89–90, 98; settlement of, 61, 90; slavery permitted in, 67; as South Carolina buffer, 64, 126n25

Grant, James: Anglo-Cherokee War and, 69, 94–96, 112; as Governor of East Florida, 87, 89, 91; Indian Johnson and, 87, 92–96; as indigo grower, 89, 91; as indigo promoter, 91; Laurens and, 87, 89, 91–96; Mount Oswald Plantation and, 87, 91, 96; Oswald and, 87, 91, 96–97

Indian Johnson: conduct and, 92–93; ethnicity and, 92, 96; Florida backcountry and, 87, 95; Grant and, 87, 92–96; Laurens and, 87, 92–97; Mount Oswald Plantation and, 87–88, 90, 92–94, 96–97; Oswald and, 87, 90, 94, 97; as overseer, 87, 92, 94–97; as possible cultivator, 98

Indians, American: attire and, 1, 5–6, 24–34, 36–38, 40–42, 68, 83, 111, 119n19, 119n20; as cultivators, 7, 75, 93–96; debt and, 63, 67, 70–71; in deerskin trade, 25, 30, 50, 62, 67, 69, 75, 88, 94, 119n20; diplomacy and, 36, 69, 95; land dispossession and, 3, 4, 7, 16, 60, 65–66, 67–71, 75; reservations, 61, 63–64, 67–68, 125n19, 127n40; runaway slave catching and, 68, 90; as slaves, 4, 7, 24, 33, 61–63, 72–76, 84, 98–99, 107–8, 112, 125n7, 128n5; slaving and, 7, 62–63, 67, 74–75, 96; territory and 2–4, 7, 59, 61–62, 68–72, 75, 89, 94, 113n4; trade and, 6–7, 23–34, 37, 41, 59–65, 67–76, 88–96, 125n9, 127n40, 127n50, 128–29n19. *See also* Catawbas; Cherokees; Congarees; Creeks; Natchez; Peedees; Savannahs; Seminoles; Settlement Indians; Wappoos; Westoes; Yamassees

Indian trade, 37, 60, 62, 63, 65, 69–89, 92, 119n20, 130n5